WALK

Adventures on the Camino

MICHELLE FRASER

First published by Ultimate World Publishing 2023
Copyright © 2023 Michelle Fraser

ISBN

Paperback: 978-1-922982-70-4
Ebook: 978-1-922982-71-1

Michelle Fraser has asserted her rights under the Copyright, Designs and Patents Act 1988 to be identified as the author of this work. The information in this book is based on the author's experiences and opinions. The publisher specifically disclaims responsibility for any adverse consequences which may result from use of the information contained herein. Permission to use information has been sought by the author. Any breaches will be rectified in further editions of the book.

All rights reserved. No part of this publication may be reproduced, stored in or introduced into a retrieval system, or transmitted in any form, or by any means (electronic, mechanical, photocopying, recording or otherwise) without the prior written permission of the author. Any person who does any unauthorised act in relation to this publication may be liable to criminal prosecution and civil claims for damages. Enquiries should be made through the publisher.

Cover design: Ultimate World Publishing
Layout and typesetting: Ultimate World Publishing
Editor: Marinda Wilkinson

Ultimate World Publishing
Diamond Creek,
Victoria Australia 3089
www.writeabook.com.au

Walk is dedicated to:

My children, Clinton and Chelsea
Thank you for supporting and encouraging me. I hope I inspire you to live life like an adventure. You will always be my biggest and best achievement.

Love you heaps.

My partner Paul
Your patience, kindness, generosity and gentle guidance makes me feel safe and loved wherever I am.

Love you.

CONTENTS

Introduction: The Good, The Bad, The Amazing	1
Chapter 1: Saint-Jean-Pied-de-Port	5
Chapter 2: The Pyrenees Mountains	15
Chapter 3: Roncesvalles to Zubiri	27
Chapter 4: Zubiri to Pamplona	35
Chapter 5: Pamplona to Puente La Reina	41
Chapter 6: Peuenta La Reina to Estella	49
Chapter 7: Estella to Los Arcos	53
Chapter 8: Los Arcos to Logrono	61
Chapter 9: Logrono to Najera	67
Chapter 10: Najera to Granon	73
Chapter 11: Granon To Villafranca Montes de Oca	79
Chapter 12: Villafranca to Burgos	85
Chapter 13: Burgos to Hontanas	89
Chapter 14: Hontanas to Boadilla del Camino	95
Chapter 15: Boadilla del Camino to Villalcazar	101
Chapter 16: Villalcazar to Calzadilla	105
Chapter 17: Calzadilla to Sahagun	109
Chapter 18: Sahagun to Reliegos	113
Chapter 19: Reliegos to Virgen del Camino	119

WALK

Chapter 20: Virgen del Camino to Villares de Orbigo — 123
Chapter 21: Villares de Orbigo to Astorga — 129
Chapter 22: Astorga to Foncebadon — 135
Chapter 23: Foncebadon to Ponferrada — 141
Chapter 24: Ponferrada to Villafranca del Bierzo — 149
Chapter 25: Villafranca del Bierzo to Herrerias — 153
Chapter 26: Herrerias To Triacastela — 157
Chapter 27: Triacastela to Barbadelo — 165
Chapter 28: Barbadelo to Gonzar — 169
Chapter 29: Gonzar to Melide — 173
Chapter 30: Melide to O Pedrouzo — 177
Chapter 31: O Pedrouzo to Santiago de Compostela — 181
Chapter 32: Santiago de Compostela to Finisterre — 185
Chapter 33: Finisterre — 189
About the Author — 193
Speaker Bio — 195
Reflections — 197

INTRODUCTION

THE GOOD, THE BAD, THE AMAZING

*'And then
There is the most dangerous risk of all –
Not doing what you want
On the bet that you can buy yourself
The freedom to do it later.'*
Randy Komisar

I did it. I am no superwoman but I have walked nearly 850 kilometres across the top of Spain. Starting in France, I crossed the Pyrenees Mountains, followed the Camino Frances Way, finishing on the shores of the Atlantic Ocean. Phew! Ask me how, and all I can say is that I just kept going. Every day, every hour, every minute. Town to town, kilometre by kilometre, step by step. This walk was a confusing combination of confidence, exhaustion, pain, happiness, wonder, tears, elation and resilience. Despite the mix of emotions and physical dilemmas, I spent 32 days marvelling at the wonder of nature and for the first time in my life, I lived, really lived, in the moment.

WALK

The Camino is achievable for everyone. It won't matter how fit you are or whether you are young or old, the Camino will challenge every individual in one way or another. My advice is to do it your way. Don't be misled into thinking there is a right or a wrong way to go about this walk. My decision to solo walk this Camino was the best one for me. However, while I was being independent, to be able to remain that way, I had to learn to ask for help when needed and accept help when it was offered. This is not something I am usually comfortable with. I have always preferred people to believe that I am capable and strong and have always been more likely to give help rather than ask for it. If you plan to walk with someone, the relationship may be tested. Some pilgrims struggle with their travelling companions despite being in close relationships, while others flourish. New relationships and friendships may be formed. These may last just for the duration of the Camino walk, or for a lifetime.

It is difficult to describe exactly how the Camino walk affected me. It was an extraordinary adventure. It challenged my thoughts about myself and also confirmed others. It played havoc with, but also strengthened, my body and my spirit. I returned home with a newfound sense of peace and contentment. My energy was refocused on many things I didn't think I could do or had time to do. I now consider the difference between what I 'should' achieve and what I 'want' to achieve. I have learned to cut myself some slack and make decisions that are reasonable, even if that means I no longer do what others expect from me.

I wrote this book so I could share 'the good, the bad and the amazing' parts of my Camino. If you are planning to walk the Camino you should be prepared that the picture you have in your mind before you start may not include all of the challenges you will face. Since walking the Camino, many people have commented

The Good, The Bad, The Amazing

they could not do the walk for so many different reasons. Mostly, it's because they are reserved or afraid, believe they are not fit enough or feel too old for adventures. If you are experiencing any of these thoughts, don't let them stop you. I know that you can do this, because I did.

When you walk the Camino, it is an individual journey. No two experiences can or should ever be the same. So, let me share my journey with you. I hope it inspires you to reach for your goals and embark on your own adventure, whether it is the Camino or something else. Whether it is solo or with friends.

You will be rewarded in so many ways. Many of these rewards will be hidden treasures that are hard to describe to someone else. Those moments will become precious experiences that are deeply personal and etched in everlasting memory.

Don't wait. Find a way and do it. You will be forever humbled by your achievement.

CHAPTER 1

SAINT-JEAN-PIED-DE-PORT

FRANCE

*'You will end up exactly
where you need to be.'*
Unknown

My flight path had taken me from Brisbane via Singapore to Frankfurt and then onto Pamplona in Spain. The date was September 22, 2019. As the plane wheels hit the runway, I felt a surge of nerves, acutely aware that I was about to enter a world of unfamiliar experiences. I tentatively followed other passengers into the airport.

While waiting for my bag, I felt intimidated by the travellers around me. Judging by the number of backpacks on the carousel, there were about thirty other pilgrims collecting their gear as well. Amongst the animated crowd, was a group of ladies, wearing matching T-shirts with a printed team name on the front. On the back was a list of the two previous Caminos they had walked. I tried to blend in with these experienced trekkers by presenting myself as a calm and composed pilgrim who was prepared to roll into adventure at a moment's notice, but I wondered if, instead, it was obvious that I was a nervous pilgrim imposter, unprepared and oblivious to the hidden mysteries of this trek. The probable reality was, that in their own excitement, they hadn't even noticed me.

I hadn't seen my backpack and boots since I left Brisbane. I had been diligently training in my boots for months and my backpack was carefully selected. They were protectively packed in a big, old suitcase with a pink bow tied securely to the handle. There was also a thoroughly procured range of essential items inside that I thought would be necessary for the next month. Without these valuable items, my Camino walk would be off to a challenging start. I was relieved when I spotted the pink bow on the carousel. I moved swiftly to claim my priceless suitcase and leave the excited chit-chat behind me.

I had pre-booked a taxi to take me to the border town of Saint-Jean-Pied-de-Port in France. It was an expensive way to travel, but it meant I was going to go straight to where I needed to be, which in my travel fatigued state, made it worth every dollar. My taxi driver was Fleur. I met her at the front of the airport and wheeled my suitcase over to the car she led me to. Fleur helped me lift my suitcase into the boot and I promptly went around and sat in the front seat. I thought it a little strange when Fleur followed me to my seat. The minute I sat down with the steering wheel in front of me, I realised why Fleur was standing beside my car door. I grinned with embarrassment and said, 'I guess you don't want me to drive.' She smiled back and shook her head. I hopped out and walked around to the other side of the car to the passenger seat. Once we were both settled in our correct positions, our drive to France commenced.

Fleur was from Columbia but had been living in Pamplona for many years. She eagerly pointed out some landmarks as we drove out of the city. There was a spot where the Camino path crossed the highway and there was a group of pilgrims stopped here. I imagined myself at that same resting spot very soon but the distance we had covered in a one and half hour taxi ride today, would probably take me three days to cover while walking.

It was a very bendy road and the gentle swaying motion of the car started to lull me into sleep. It took all the determination I had left to stay awake as we rounded the many curves of the beautiful Pyrenees Mountain Range. To keep myself alert, I chatted enthusiastically, asking as many questions as I could think of, to prevent sleep prevailing. We talked about Fleur's life in Columbia and why she had moved to Spain. She told me about different aspects of the Spanish culture she either enjoyed or found unusual.

After 32 hours of travel, I finally arrived at my hotel. I thanked Fleur for her safe delivery of me, retrieved my suitcase from the boot, and went inside. The man in the reception greeted me in French. He found my booking and gave me details about dinner served in the restaurant tonight. I didn't think I would be awake for dinner but I thanked him anyway. I took my room key and headed towards the staircase. I stopped and looked for the lift. There wasn't one. The rickety old wooden staircase was the only way up. I released a sigh that was probably way too loud and reluctantly headed up four flights of stairs with my suitcase in tow. Thankfully, there was no-one else around to witness my huffing and puffing. At the very top, at the end of the hallway, I found my room.

WALK

I opened the door and entered into a cosy room. There were two single beds with light green covers in one room and another single bed in a kind of sleep out area. A bright green wooden table was in the middle of the room and a striped antique style seat faced to a window that overlooked the rooftops and allowed a clear view of the Pyrenees Mountains. These pieces of furniture gave the room a quaint and rustic French atmosphere.

Despite feeling exhausted (little did I know that there was another level of exhaustion that I was to experience the next day), I unpacked my suitcase on the spare single bed. I separated all my gear into groups ready to re-pack them into my backpack for tomorrow's departure. I intended to leave the old suitcase behind in the room. Searching the hotel for a washing machine was more effort than I was willing to engage in, so I washed my travelling clothes while I showered. I was delighted to find a hairdryer. This was a luxury I wasn't expecting to come across in the upcoming days. When I was satisfied that I was organised and had everything I needed in my fold-out backpack, I headed off on a self-guided tour of the town.

The first stop was the Pilgrim Office. Here I received my Pilgrim Passport *(Credencial)* and my first stamp. A Pilgrim Passport gets stamped at accommodation and bars along the way. You must have a passport to allow you to stay at 'pilgrim only' accommodation called an albergue. It also allows you to claim your *Compostela* at the end. The *Compostela* is a certificate of completion to prove that you have walked the Camino, provided you have walked at least the last 100 kilometres. You can request this from the Pilgrim Office in Santiago. The lady who assisted me also gave me a map, a list of albergues and some good advice about the Camino Frances. This was the route that I would be taking from here to Santiago. For the cost of a donation, I chose a scallop shell, out of a wooden

Saint-Jean-Pied-de-Port

box, to hang from my backpack and identify me as a pilgrim. The scallop shell is a symbol of the Camino but there was no formal reason to be identified. It is just part of the pilgrim tradition.

Next on the agenda was the citadel. This is the highest point in town. I planned to take some photos and film my first video from here. I had decided to document my walk with both photos and video and intended to post on Facebook and Instagram. I was definitely not a skilled social media user.

Looking out from the citadel, I could see the size of the town. The Pyrenees Mountains formed a lush, bright green backdrop. It was remarkably busy up here and I felt awkward setting up my camera to take selfies and film myself. I knew I should stop worrying about what others were thinking. There were plenty of tourists and pilgrims doing the same thing. After several attempts to film an introductory video, I was satisfied that I had something I was happy to share, so I packed up and headed down the hill to explore the rest of the town.

Saint-Jean-Pied-de-Port is a beautiful little village in France at the base of the Pyrenees Mountains. The main street is paved with cobblestones and lined with bright flowers and greenery. It was alive with pilgrims and tourists. Most people seemed to be in groups or with at least a partner. I unexpectedly felt a dash of loneliness on my own, but I prompted myself to remember my silent quest for independence.

There were signs of the Camino everywhere with scallop shells and yellow arrows on doorways and posts, hostels advertising cheap pilgrim rooms, shops with Camino mementos, and plenty of people walking around with backpacks. If you needed any trekking gear, you could readily buy it. There were bakeries and cafes dispensing strong wafts of coffee into the street and cabinets filled with delicious looking pastries. I walked by a spice shop and was drawn in by the wonderful smells. I explored other shops but buying anything was out of the question. I definitely didn't need to add any additional weight to my backpack.

I walked past a church and went inside to take a look. It was as dark and silent as you would expect in a very old church. I settled on a seat and looked around at the stained glass and the architecture. The melancholic atmosphere of the church made me feel sad. When the candle stand was vacant, I went over and took two candles from the box. I lit them and placed them on the rack. One candle was for my Dad who had passed away recently. I fondly remembered how Dad would lean forward and listen intently when I told him a story. He was always interested and curious and he listened like he had never heard anything like it before. I was mindful that after this adventure, I was not going to be able to share my story with Dad. I reflected with gratitude on all that Dad had done for me and thanked him. The second candle was for the good health and happiness of my family, friends and colleagues. I said an affirmation for everyone back at home to remain safe and well while I was away.

I reflected on the history of the church and imagined the many pilgrims who would have visited here before starting their own journey. I acknowledged with appreciation that I had the luxury and privilege of both time and health to be able to walk the Camino. I contemplated the upcoming weeks and steadied my imagination about how this might unfold. I sat for a long time with the silence wrapped around me, lost in my thoughts. Finally, it was time to put an end to this solitude and reflection and return to the outside light, fresh air and noise of the street.

Saint-Jean-Pied-de-Port

I was hungry and keen to find something to eat. Further up the road, I walked past a delicatessen selling salami and cheese. On the footpath was a board advertising a cheese and ham bocadilla (a traditional Spanish sandwich made with a crusty baguette) accompanied with a bottle of water. This was tempting so I went inside.

A burly looking man with a black apron came to the counter and I asked for the sandwich advertised on the board. It was obvious by the shrugging of his shoulders that he did not understand me, and he seemed a little frustrated with my lack of French. I had been learning to speak some Spanish for this walk but not any French. I walked back towards the door and pointed to his sign. He nodded his head and walked out to the kitchen.

While he was making my sandwich, I strolled around the shop admiring the large selection of dried meat and the big wheels of cheese. I love cheese so I particularly enjoyed looking at the variety on display. I imagined how good it would taste. I briefly contemplated asking the man for some cheese to take with me but thought that I might make him angry again if I couldn't convey that I wanted just a small piece rather than one of the large wheels. As the cheese debate played out in my head, the man returned with my sandwich and bottle of water. He gave me a second paper bag with a delicious looking pastry in it. He must have forgiven me for not speaking French. I thanked him and was glad I had not tempted fate and ruined his generosity by asking for cheese.

I took my bocadilla and walked back to the river. I sat on the stone wall of the river and did some 'people watching' while I ate my sandwich. I wondered what their stories might be and why they were here. I predicted that I would hear some of those stories over the next month as we met up and walked to our common destination.

I re-wrapped half the bocadilla for later, just in case I was hungry before bed, and left the river and walked to the starting point of the Camino. I was going to be leaving Saint-Jean early in the morning and I wanted to be sure I was not going to get lost and waste valuable time on the first day. I decided to take a selfie in case it was too dark in the morning to record my departure. It took way too long to set up the camera and then too much misused time constantly looking around for a moment when I had no-one watching me. That moment never eventuated so I just had to smile and get on with it. I took numerous photos of myself before I had one I was happy with. I walked back to my hotel, carefully tracing my steps, so I could easily find my way back in the morning.

I had forgotten about the four flights of stairs to reach my bedroom and with another sigh, I headed back up them thankful that I was not carrying my suitcase this time. Back in my hotel room, I packed my backpack for Day 1. I tried it on to check how it felt. It is recommended your backpack weighs about 7 kilograms. I thought I had the weight sorted before I left home, but now I wasn't so sure. The last-minute items I had put in may have added more weight than I thought. I adjusted the straps and continued to fuss for a while before I was sure everything was ready.

While I was doing this rearranging and adjusting, the sky had darkened and clouds had moved in. I checked the weather forecast. Tomorrow was going to be rainy. All day. It had not rained today. It hadn't rained for weeks and it wasn't going to rain the day after I left. But it was going to rain tomorrow for my first day on the Camino. Oh well, I thought, bring it on. I am brave, tough and ready. Knowing that it was going to rain meant that at least I

Saint-Jean-Pied-de-Port

would be prepared. I repacked my backpack with rain in mind and rearranged several items just to make sure I had quick access to rain gear and other bits and pieces I thought might be necessary.

I was ready to go. I slipped into bed. I had trouble going to sleep because I was intently alert that tomorrow was the big day. There was no turning back now. I was as ready as I could be and adventure awaited. I looked forward to whatever was ahead. Good, bad and amazing.

CHAPTER 2

THE PYRENEES MOUNTAINS

SAINT-JEAN-PIED-DE-PORT TO RONCESVALLES

DAY 1 – 24.7 KM

'My philosophy is to take one day at a time. Tomorrow is even out of sight for me.'
Bobby Darin

At 4 am I was wide awake. It was probably the result of jetlag but perhaps it was also the excitement and anticipation of the day to come. I stretched slowly and tentatively got out of bed. I looked out of the window towards the mountains I would cross today. It was very dark and it was pouring rain. At least I was expecting this.

I showered, made full use of the hairdryer, dressed in my trekking clothes, and then made a black coffee. I wouldn't normally drink

WALK

black coffee but I had no milk. I sat on the bed, cautiously sipping the piping hot coffee and pretending that I was enjoying it. While I was doing this, I stared at my backpack which was leaning against the bed. I was deliberately procrastinating about leaving. The longer I took to drink the coffee, the longer I could delay my departure.

Extending my procrastination to the limit and highly aware that this was not a useful strategy, I put down the coffee, finalised my preparation, checked I hadn't forgotten anything, and picked up my backpack. As I lifted it to my back it felt much heavier than when I did the test run last night. I shrugged it around a little and once it was clipped into position, there was nothing to do but walk out that door and down those four flights of stairs.

With all my delaying tactics, it was now 7:30 am. I had not had any breakfast but I still had my half-finished bocadilla in my bag from yesterday. I planned to eat after I had walked for a couple of hours. I headed to the reception, handed my key to the manager, and stepped outside. Apprehensively, I took the first of many steps I would take to walk approximately 850 kilometres to Santiago de Compostela and then to Finisterre. A wave of doubt came over me and for an instant, I wished there was someone with me to push me on my way.

The rain had eased a little and the first rays of light were evident. The street lights were still on and because the streets were very wet, a shimmer of gold was dispersed across them. I saw two ladies watching me as I approached the stone archway. They asked me to take a photo of them. I obliged and they reciprocated the favour. It was just like the first day of school. I stood proudly in my fresh, unsoiled uniform with a shiny new bag on my back and an eagerness to see what the day would bring. I was having

The Pyrenees Mountains

no doubts or regrets and my spirit of adventure was good to go. Walking poles at the ready, I walked through the archway and confidently strode out of town to cross the Pyrenees Mountains.

Almost immediately, the rain started again as I walked uphill on a bitumen road. I had placed my backpack cover on before I left my room but I now had to retrieve my poncho from my backpack. The concern with this was that I had to remove my backpack first. Once I had located my poncho, I then repositioned my backpack on my shoulders, pulled the poncho over my head and then tried to pull it down to go over my backpack. The poncho got stuck halfway over my head and was caught above my backpack. As much as I tried, I was unable to move my arm far enough to my back to reach and pull the poncho down. I removed the poncho and attempted again. The rainfall was increasing, and I was becoming wetter. I managed, after several further tiring attempts, to get the poncho technique sorted and it was now positioned carefully over my head and backpack. I could now resume walking up this first hill.

It wasn't long before the weight of my backpack became evident. It felt like it was 20 kg rather than 7 kg. I was extremely surprised at how slow I was walking because I thought I had done enough training. It was obvious that I was not prepared enough for the steep climbs. I reassured myself by thinking that this must be the hardest part of the day. I had a lot to learn about the Pyrenees because the hard bit was still ahead of me.

I stopped to look around. I was surrounded by beautiful green paddocks, small hills in the foreground and mountains wrapped in fog in the background. There were charming cottages and farmhouses behind wooden fences. Some close to the road and others in the distance. There were cows and sheep grazing in the paddocks across the misty countryside. The scenery

WALK

was blurry in the rain, but it added to the charm of the French country morning.

I followed a road sign and turned in to a paddock to head up another steep incline. This path was muddy and difficult to navigate over the wet rocks. A fellow pilgrim stopped as he walked past me and suggested that I take the rubber ends off my walking poles. This would leave a metal tip exposed and it would dig into the soft ground and hold. I had no idea these metal tips were even there. The helpful pilgrim stood patiently and watched me while I tried to take off the rubber ends but they were too tight and I could not budge them. I think he could see how tired I was and thankfully, he gripped the ends of the poles and, as I held the other end, he removed the rubber stops and gave them to me. This small adjustment made an enormous difference in improving my steadiness on the muddy, rocky path. It was the first of many trekking tips to learn.

Further along, I met a lady from Canada who was walking with her husband. She was in tears. I stopped and asked her if she was okay and she said that she must be crazy and did not think that she could do this. I empathised with her and I wished her well. I never saw her again so I am not sure if she continued beyond that day or she gave up when she reached Orisson.

The constant uphill walk was persistently difficult. When the rain eased, it was cold and windy. There would be none of the promised mountain views I had seen in numerous YouTube viewings because a heavy fog had descended and the views were shielded. When I reached the top of the first big hill, I did however, have a stunning view of the mountains even with the thick, white fog clinging to them. I decided now was a good time for a selfie. As I started to set up my equipment, a pilgrim stopped and asked if I would like

The Pyrenees Mountains

him to take my photo. I eagerly accepted his offer so that I didn't have to set up the camera stand. We spoke briefly. He was walking with his wife who was slightly ahead of him. I thanked him and we wished each other *'Buen Camino'*, a common greeting or farewell said between pilgrims which means 'good way'.

After four hours and eight very gruelling kilometres of mud, rain and hills, I arrived at Orisson. I saw the pilgrim cafe on the side of the mountain through a blanket of fog. I am not sure if it was overwhelm or relief that created a slight quiver in my voice, but the words 'I am saved', were uttered out loud. I was relieved to be there and so grateful that I was. I was looking forward to taking off my backpack, going to the bathroom and getting something hot to eat. The fog had enveloped the building which housed the cafe. Some pilgrims stay here overnight and continue the walk to Roncesvalles the next day.

I had originally planned to stop before Orisson to enjoy my half-eaten bocadilla. The constant rain, my inexperience in removing and putting back on my poncho, the weight of taking off and re-lifting my backpack, and the wet and muddy ground had put a decisive end to that brilliant plan. Other than the black coffee I had early this morning, I hadn't eaten anything. I was extremely thankful I had a water bladder so I could at least sip water as I walked.

I stepped into the cafe at Orisson. The floor was wet and the room was loud from the volume of many pilgrims crammed in and talking excitedly while they ate their meal. On a clear day, seating outside showcases the extraordinary views, but sitting out there today was out of the question. I stood just inside the doorway with my backpack and poncho still on, doing my bit to contribute to the wet floor. I scanned for a table and there didn't seem to even be a single spare seat. This was an agonising situation for an introvert. To delay the inevitable torture of joining a group of pilgrims I didn't know, I left my backpack and poncho on while I ordered my food. I asked for a vegetable soup which was promptly put on the counter.

Aware of the wet floor, I carefully carried the soup and walked across the floor. I spied with undeniable relief, an empty table back near the doorway. I placed the soup bowl on the table. I now had to take my poncho and backpack off. I was nervous because my inexperience in orchestrating a smooth transition had been evident this morning. I struggled out of my poncho trying not to swing my arms around too wildly while raising it over my backpack and above my head. I then lifted my backpack off my shoulders. As I swung it around to place it on the floor, the weight caused it to free flow and it caught on a chair. The chair went flying backward and it felt like the whole room stopped talking and looked at me. Without any additional fuss, I casually picked up the chair and slid onto it with only one sneaky glance to see if everyone was still watching me. Luckily, the bowl of soup I had placed on the table was not caught up in the drama.

Within a minute, a couple of other pilgrims joined me at my table. Beth was 24 and from Alaska. She had only decided three weeks ago to walk the Camino in between jobs. JT also sat with us. He was a young man, about 22, who was on a backpacking adventure around the world. He had an enormous 'everything but the kitchen sink' type backpack. When he walked past me later in the day, he strode out as if there was no weight at all on his back. I was impressed and envious of his strength and youth. Last to join us was Jimmy. Jimmy was American and was realising his ambition to walk the Camino. We fell easily into conversation while we ate our lunch. They were my first pilgrim friends. I never believed I

The Pyrenees Mountains

could be so happy to have company. It was great to share some conversation about our experience so far.

I savoured my soup and made sure that every spoonful was scrapped from the bowl. Given that I had been very slow for this first part of the day and I was not yet halfway, I decided that I had better get going. After a quick bathroom stop, I tackled the backpack and poncho again. This time, I was smart enough to ask a fellow pilgrim walking by to pull my poncho down over my backpack. I was not wanting to cause a second scene in the cafe. I decided then, that while I was going to embrace my independence, if I needed help, I would ask for it. Being independent does not mean doing everything on your own. It means having the good sense to recognise when you need help and be courageous enough to ask for or accept it when it is needed. This decision was going to serve me well on many occasions throughout my walk.

The next 17 kilometres took me across the top of the Pyrenees. The landscape was stunning and I took in every detail. I felt a sense of limitless freedom in the wide-open spaces on top of these mountains. I was mesmerised by the majestic griffon vultures. Some stood like statues on the rocky outcrops and watched me approach while others were soaring around me with wingspans reaching as much as 3 metres. They were searching for small animals to snack on. At one point, a number of them appeared to be circling me, and given my weariness, I wondered if they could sense my inclination to lie down and give in to the tiredness, rain, wind, fog and unending steep inclines. If you are thinking about doing this walk, do some uphill training. There are very large vultures waiting for you to drop.

I saw mountain horses, sheep and goats. The horses were big and healthy and the goats had huge horns and looked quite mean.

WALK

The goats were close to the path so I hesitantly walked past them thinking that if they were to charge, it was over for me. There was no way that I could defend myself or move any faster than I was. My walking had become more like a drag of the feet rather than the glorious trek I had envisioned it would be.

Despite my weariness, I was nonetheless mobilised by the realisation that I was crossing the vast expanse of the Pyrenees Mountains all by myself. It was surreal to think that after a year of planning and preparation, I was right there doing what I set out to do. I think it was the first time, I had ever experienced fully living in the moment. My eyes soaked in all that there was to see and my lungs worked overtime inhaling every ounce of the fresh air. I turned in circles to the see the view before, behind and beside me. I did not want to miss anything. I probably added at least an extra hour to my day by taking a considerable collection of photos and videos.

The Pyrenees Mountains

Towards the end of the day, I met up with the Polish man who had taken my photo. He was with his wife and she was quite distressed as she had run out of water. I had an unopened bottle that I offered to her. She didn't want to take it, but I insisted. She suggested I pour some water into her hand and keep the bottle but I had a water bladder in my backpack and it still had sufficient water for me. She was most grateful and we walked and talked for a short time before they went on ahead.

At this stage, I was beyond weary. I was starting to think that I may be the very last pilgrim left out here in the middle of nowhere. Many pilgrims had passed me during the day including my lunch friends from Orisson. I sat on a rock for a small rest break and finally ate a squashed plum and my half bocadilla (yes, I had kept it just in case). I surveyed the area for a suitable spot to shelter if I couldn't keep going. With no promising options, I had to get up and tread onward.

I had been advised by the lady at the Pilgrim's Office to take the slightly longer path into Roncesvalles as the alternate path, while shorter, was very steep and dangerous. I decided that being the first day, and there may not be anyone behind me, that I would take the good advice given and be a responsible hiker. This essentially added almost half a kilometre to my walk. That doesn't seem like much unless you had already walked 11 hours and you can barely move your legs to keep going. I contemplated whether I had made the right decision while the last few kilometres seemed to stretch out and transform into an endless exasperating march.

When I arrived in Roncesvalles it was 7:22 pm. It was 12 hours since I had started walking. Thankfully, I had booked a room in anticipation that I would be tired and want privacy at the end of the day. That was exactly what I wanted when I finally dragged myself to the guesthouse. I limped into the lobby feeling sick. I asked for my reservation and took out my Pilgrim Passport to get a stamp. It was wet and crumpled so I just held it instead. There would be plenty more opportunities to get it stamped.

I graciously took my room key and walked through the reception door. To my horror, there was a staircase, and my room was on the second floor. It was all I could do to not sit on the bottom stair and start crying. I roused myself up for one last effort and dragged my aching body up four half-size flights of stairs. I found my room halfway along the corridor and struggled to turn the key in the lock. When I pushed on the door, it flung open and I collapsed into the open space in the doorway.

I untangled my backpack from my arms, left it on the floor and headed straight to the bathroom. There was a shower over the bath but I honestly didn't think I had the strength to stand. There was no bath plug in sight. I plugged the drain with my sock and proceeded to get into the warm water with my clothes. I washed them at the same time as myself. I cleaned my teeth, located my phone charger, had a couple of glasses of water, and crawled into bed. I fell to sleep instantly. No Camino jobs were completed that evening. I gave no thought to dinner or preparation for the next day. Honestly, I wasn't even sure I was going to make it to the next day.

I would easily describe Day 1 as torturous. It took me 12 hours to walk across the Pyrenees. I reached an altitude of 1450 m. Despite what I thought was a rigorous training schedule, I was physically unprepared for the experience of that day. My backpack was not sitting correctly and was too heavy. The rain made the walk muddy and tiring. My feet were sore but thankfully, not from blisters. All day I had focused on steps rather than kilometres. When I did

The Pyrenees Mountains

search into the distance, it seemed impossible that I would reach the end. I set small goals and as I reached each one I set the next one. I had to constantly tell myself, 'You've got this. Do not give up. Keep going. You're getting closer.' My inner cheerleader was working overtime.

That night, I was too exhausted to recognise what I had just achieved. I had never done anything as physically difficult. Looking back on this first day, I appreciate that what I did that day was awesome and courageous. I crossed the Pyrenees Mountains and I am so proud of myself. I am thankful for the experience but even more thankful that I finished alive.

CHAPTER 3

RONCESVALLES TO ZUBIRI

DAY 2 – 22 KM

*'You don't always need a plan.
Sometimes you just need to breathe,
trust, let go and see what happens.'*
Unknown

I was starving when I woke up in the morning. To my amazement, I had very few aches and pains. I stretched my limbs, feet and back. I showered and washed my hair and then rubbed some sports cream into my calves. I headed downstairs to the dining room for breakfast. As I took each step down, I was recalling the painful determination it took yesterday to walk up these stairs. I was a little nervous going into the dining room on my own. There was a group of eight pilgrims seated at a big round table right at the doorway. They were excitedly chatting to each other and

WALK

I guessed it might have been about their successful crossing of the Pyrenees. Seeing them eating breakfast together provided a fleeting reminder that I was all on my own.

I headed straight to the buffet table and poured an orange juice. Despite waking up hungry, I now did not feel like eating much so I took a vanilla yoghurt and two pastries. I sat and read my guide book while I ate and drank my hot cup of tea. I grabbed a banana and an apple from the table to put in my backpack for later and went back up to my room, via the dreaded stairs, for final preparations for the day's walk.

It wasn't a difficult task to pack this morning as I had not removed very much from my backpack. The clothes that I had washed last night were slightly damp so I packed them into a 'dry' bag. I pinned my damp socks on the outside of my backpack so they would dry as I walked. Socks hanging from my backpack would become a regular routine.

I located a dry pair of socks and put on my boots. There were no blisters and I felt enormously relieved for that. I filled my water bladder and placed it on the outside of my backpack between the pack and the straps. It is not the normal place to carry a water bladder but it sat nicely here and I could then avoid the risk of it leaking into my bag. I put my phone in its holder, the GoPro in my pocket and with timidity swung the backpack on my back. It weighed me down immediately. I adjusted the straps again, in the hope it would fit better today. I took one last look around the room to ensure that I had left nothing behind and then tackled that staircase and stepped out to the adventure of Day 2.

It was already 8:30 am. I had a quick look around Roncesvalles. I hadn't cared at all about seeing it yesterday when I shuffled

Roncesvalles to Zubiri

to my hotel and this morning I didn't want to waste too much time before I was on my way. Right at the start of the trail was a large sign saying 790 kilometres to Santiago de Compostela. It is a popular spot for a pilgrim photo. I waited patiently while two female pilgrims took a photo of each other. As I started to retrieve my selfie stick, one of the ladies asked if I would like her to take my photo. I accepted and thanked her.

WALK

The Camino path immediately headed into dimly lit woods. It was dense with canopy trees, thick, green bushes and undergrowth. This area was said to be a place of witchcraft in the 16th century. The story told is that nine women were put to death in the forest between Roncesvalles and Burguete after they were accused of witchcraft. The darkness, moist ground and damp smells contributed to the feeling that this is a place of misfortune and mystery. After being out in the open weather yesterday, walking under a canopy of trees was a pleasant way to start the day. Several pilgrims passed me as I slowly wandered through the woods enjoying the coolness of mother nature and taking lots of photos and video.

As I walked, I attempted several times, to film a recap video about my day on the Pyrenees. Each time I started speaking, I was reduced to tears. After the brutal initiation into Camino trekking yesterday, I was still extremely emotional each time I thought about what I had experienced and accomplished. By the time I reached the end of the woods, I had managed to reign in the emotions and recount my epic adventure over the Pyrenees.

After about 7 kilometres, I came to the small town of Espinal. I was needing a bathroom stop so I detoured into the first cafe I saw. I participated in some light chatter with a couple of female pilgrims as we waited our turn. Feeling confident, I headed out of town thinking I now had this hiking business under control.

I was barely five minutes up the street when from across the road, I heard an elderly lady call out to me. I stopped and turned to her. She asked if I was walking the Camino. I smiled and proudly said yes but thought surely it was obvious with this backpack hitched on. She smiled back at me. 'That's not the way. You have to go back there,' she said pointing behind me to a street on the

Roncesvalles to Zubiri

left which went out to a laneway. I had missed the turn and the guiding yellow arrow. I felt embarrassed but was so pleased she had called out. Imagine if I had kept heading up that street. Who knows how long I would have walked before I realised my error. Hoping no-one else had noticed my detour, I sheepishly waved to the lady to thank her. I crossed the road where she had pointed and headed up the laneway to the road where I was supposed to be.

It was a beautiful sunny day. I was in a T-shirt today and enjoying the warm weather after wearing my poncho all day yesterday. I strolled past fenced, very green, grassed paddocks with sheep and cows grazing throughout. Most of the walking this morning was through woodland on relatively flat sections. The paths were a mixture of paving, leaf-covered dirt, rocks and concrete and many of them were under the cool canopy of trees. It was shaded and I was feeling relaxed. I walked full of admiration and breathed in the peace and fresh air.

Despite my exhaustion from yesterday, I was walking at a good pace however, my pace appeared to be slower than most others. I was often overtaken. I was not sure if I was recovering from yesterday or I had a false sense of my fitness. All the pilgrims I had met so far, had given kind words of encouragement as they passed by me. At this early stage of the Camino, there was a general conversation about what country we were from, how we were feeling and further discussions about any highlights so far. We always wished each other a *'Buen Camino'* as we parted. My impression was that no-one was more important than another. We were all pilgrims heading to one destination.

Towards the end of the day, panic about accommodation for the evening started to creep in. I hadn't made a booking for tonight. As I walked, my brain was checking off all the possible unfortunate scenarios if I was unable to secure accommodation. One of them was that I might have to keep walking past Zubiri to the next town. This was unimaginable at this stage of the day. A more appealing solution would be to unroll my sleeping bag and sleep under a tree. These 'what if' thoughts consumed me for quite some time. Eventually, I decided that the time and energy spent on worry was pointless and I should wait until I arrived in Zubiri then decide what to do next.

The walk into Zubiri was a steep, downhill dirt track. Stepping around the many loose rocks made it a tiring challenge. The path became rougher and rockier and harder to navigate as it continued to track downhill. Pilgrims could easily come to grief in this area if they lost their balance. Days after I had walked this part, I heard that a pilgrim had been airlifted by helicopter from here after they fell.

I arrived in Zubiri at 2:30 pm. I approached the first two pilgrims I saw to ask if they had any accommodation suggestions. They said the place where they were staying was full. I looked to my left and saw a couple of guesthouses. I tried each of these but they were also full. I headed over the old stone bridge into town and continued, without luck, trying other places. I was tired, downcast and wondering why I hadn't booked something. Those 'what if' thoughts were rapidly creeping back.

I watched a lady approach me as I neared the centre of town. In a mixture of Spanish and English, she asked if I was looking for a room. I said yes. She said she had a room available at her place. I asked if it was a single room with a bathroom. She had difficulty understanding and after a series of attempts at communicating with each other, I nodded my head and said yes. I wasn't really sure what I had agreed to.

Roncesvalles to Zubiri

The lady indicated for me to follow her and she led me to an apartment building. I was glad to see a lift and we went up to the third floor. Her apartment had been redesigned into three guest rooms. My room had two single beds. There was a shared bathroom. The lady gave me towels and pointed to the shampoo and other toiletries that I was welcome to use. She took me into the kitchen and demonstrated how I could wash my clothes in the sink and then hang them out to dry on the patio. She took my payment in cash, stamped my Pilgrim Passport and left me to it.

There were chores to do and no matter how tired I was today, they must be done. The list included shower, laundry, dinner, gathering snacks, taking care of feet and sore muscles, charging batteries, reading the guidebook, and editing photos and videos to post on social media.

First was the shower. It was wonderfully warm and relaxing. It felt like a luxury to wash and dry my hair. I washed my clothes in the kitchen sink as the lady had shown me and hung them up outside on a plastic rope line. The line hung over the patio and I was concerned that the wind would blow my clothes off and they would end up on the pavement below. I made sure each piece of clothing was secured with several pegs each just to be sure.

Once again, I was too tired to eat or go and stock up on food. I had some snacks leftover from the day so I knew I would be set for the morning. Before going to bed I collected my half-dried clothes from the outside line. I hung them around my room on door handles, chairs and bed heads so they would continue drying during the night. I repacked my backpack as much as possible and had everything laid out and ready for the morning. I wanted to get an early start. I edited my video from the day and, content with what I had done, I switched off the lights and went to sleep.

CHAPTER 4

ZUBIRI TO PAMPLONA

DAY 3 – 21 KM

'An early morning walk is a blessing for the whole day.'
Henry David Thoreau

I had a comfortable and peaceful sleep last night, so I easily packed up and departed Zubiri just before daybreak. I walked back through town, over the stone bridge, to the Camino path and hiked to the top of the first hill. I turned and looked back on the town. It was dark except for the random pattern of street and house lights. Standing in the fading darkness, taking in this view and hearing the birds twittering their morning song, was satisfying. I welcomed and appreciated the new day.

Today the path guided me through a mixture of pasture, mountain range and forest. On one of the forest paths, I was passed by a man leading a laden donkey in the opposite direction. I thought that maybe he was a pilgrim on the return journey. There was

WALK

no opportunity to communicate as he didn't look up as he went by me.

I was excited to come across my first wild blackberry bushes. I felt like I had discovered edible gold and I eagerly picked a handful as a sweet treat. I saw other bushes that could have been blueberries but I was not sure so I was cautious and left them alone.

Walking into the first village, I stopped suddenly in my tracks when I saw a large dog lazing in the sunlight on the edge of the road. If I had brought one fear with me, this was it. Dogs. My fear of dogs always generated a rush of adrenalin causing me to walk out of my way to avoid them. There was no way around this dog if I wanted to continue walking. I braced myself. Now was the time to be brave and to my relief, the dog continued laying on the side of the road, showing no interest in me as I stepped quietly and cautiously past him.

In the next village, I walked past an old man sweeping the paved street outside his home. He greeted me with a *'Buenos Dias'* which means 'good morning or good day'. He pointed to my backpack and continued to speak in Spanish. I didn't understand any other words so he might have been telling me my backpack looked too heavy. If that was the case, I was in total agreeance with him. I nodded my head and waved my hand to confirm that his observation was spot on.

The path followed the Arga River for most of the morning. Occasionally, I heard vehicles travelling on the highway not far away from me. My focus was on the sounds of the river which were relaxing and comforting. I imagined its many personalities being revealed through the rhythm of the water as it flowed confidently and then sometimes gingerly along the banks. It

Zubiri to Pamplona

alternated between being playful and happy, composed and peaceful, hurried and busy, and calm and restful. To my delight, the little birds that had greeted me this morning seemed to be following me, and I told myself that their song was wishing me safe travels. It was comforting to have both the river and the birds accompany me and shape a day of perfection in nature.

As I came out of the woods, there was a cafe filled with pilgrims. It was time to stop and get something to eat. The other pilgrims were greeting each other like long lost friends and I looked around to see if there was anyone familiar to me. There was not. I guessed they had all met each other in an Albergue or were travelling in a group. Being a true introvert, I was not about to insert myself into any of these groups so I found my own table and set down my backpack. I went inside to the bathroom and then ordered a piece of egg tart and a coffee. I enjoyed my break but as soon as I finished eating, I gathered my gear and got back on the trail.

Later in the day, I came to the bottom of a big hill. I looked up to see the very steep climb I had to make to get to the top. I braced myself to carry the weight of my backpack up this dirt path and reluctantly started on my way. I was probably not much more than a third of the way up when I heard a whirring sound and out of nowhere, a mountain bike rider came tearing down the hill towards me. I moved swiftly to the edge of the path and let him go by. I was a little shaken and wondered why he wouldn't be riding with more care in anticipation that someone would be walking up the hill. I checked to make sure there wasn't a second bike coming down before I continued. I did not enjoy a single bit of this hill climb. It was hot, tiring and hard on my muscles. It felt like the weight of my backpack was pulling me backward and slowing down my efforts to gain ground. It was the first big challenge since the Pyrenees climb. With the hill climb accomplished, the rest of the day passed by without any stand-out moments and I was pleased when I could see the city of Pamplona in the distance. I felt tired and was ready to stop walking.

Pamplona is the first city along the Frances route. I was staying in the old part of the city which was surrounded by a big stone wall. It was a long walk to the entry gate and I dragged my tired body along. Even though this was where I arrived a couple of days earlier, I did not have my bearings. I walked around for some time looking for my accommodation before I was compelled to ask for directions to avoid wasting any more time. I was glad to find my hotel and even more glad that there was a lift up to my room. I packed myself into the tiny lift and went up to my small but comfortable room.

After showering and organising my gear, I started to arrange some items in a pile to post home. At the last minute, I convinced myself that I might need these items and decided to keep them just in case. In hindsight, this was a big mistake. It was unnecessary weight and I would have been better off without it. There was no need to carry extra items I was unlikely to use. There were plenty of shops that had anything I might need. It was a couple of unnecessarily taxing weeks before I learned this lesson and in the meantime, I carried weight I didn't need to. I was able to ask myself, how often in the past have I hung on to something, just in case, to find out I never ever needed it? Since returning from the Camino, I have become more confident at letting go of things. It is always a work in progress, both physically and emotionally.

I was hungry and decided to head out to get dinner. It took a while to settle on where to eat but I found a restaurant advertising a pilgrim's meal. A pilgrim's meal is three courses and costs around 10 Euros. I ordered my meal and asked for a beer to go with it. I sat

Zubiri to Pamplona

outside the restaurant in the plaza and while I waited for the first course, I observed everyday Spanish life in the city. I ate most of the first course of rice and one chicken wing from the second and that was it. The basket of bread and fried potato chips were not touched. Neither was the dessert. I was full of food and feeling tired so I headed back to my room to get some well-earned sleep.

CHAPTER 5

PAMPLONA TO PUENTE LA REINA

DAY 4 – 24 KM

*'We cannot tarry here.
We must march my darlings.'*
Walt Whitman

I left Pamplona at 8:30 am. I enjoyed sleeping in. It was 15 degrees and a little overcast. I was pleased about this as I knew that I had a very big climb ahead of me today.

I was disappointed with myself this morning. I had been suffering from the weight of my backpack for three days and when I had the opportunity last night to take out all the unnecessary items and either throw them away, send them home or mail them on to Santiago, I didn't do it. A big case of 'What if ..?' hit me and I was once again frozen by fear of the unknown. 'What if I need it

WALK

later?' was not a valid excuse for continuing to carry items I could purchase if required.

The sleeping bag had been number one on my hit list. It was my biggest 'What if …?' My plan was not to stay in any albergues, sharing a room with unfamiliar people and sleeping in a bunk bed. So it was unlikely that I would need the sleeping bag but I hung onto it just in case. I resolved to try again tonight to declutter my backpack.

Just as it was a long walk into Pamplona it was a long walk out. Today I would walk up to Alto de Perdon where there is a series of metal statues, shaped in the form of pilgrims standing along the edge of the summit.

Halfway up the first hill, I found a small tree that offered some shade. I stopped, took off my backpack and sat down. I pulled out a half-eaten packet of plain potato chips and while I snacked, I watched an army of pilgrims make their way up the hill towards me. I leaned against the trunk and looked back from where I had already walked. There was an uninterrupted view bringing together the city of Pamplona, the beautiful mountain range, the brown wheat fields and the bright blue sky. I wondered about the army of pilgrims and how many might also stop to look behind them as they passed by me on this hill.

I thought about all the times I had been in a rush to get to the next goal, and neglected to stop and enjoy what I had achieved, or celebrate where I had come from. I felt guilt that in the stress of combining parenting and working, that I wasn't observant enough of my children as they grew and I wished I had watched more closely as they changed and developed. I wondered what I had missed when I just rushed into the next part of life and

Pamplona to Puente La Reina

how things might change in the future if I stopped setting shiny new goals and became content with staying in the space I was currently in. It occurred to me that when I returned home, I should reprioritise my goals and focus only on the ones that would keep me in a place of harmony and comfort and allow me the time to reflect, enjoy and celebrate what I already had. I found a degree of peace sitting under this tree, reflecting on these thoughts, and by the time I stood up to go, many of the pilgrims were well ahead of me.

When I reached the first ridge, I started to set up my selfie stand to take a photo with Pamplona behind me. A few pilgrims were resting on a bench looking at the view. It was a bit windy and I was trying to make the stand balance on its three skinny legs. A voice from the bench said, 'Would you like me to do that for you?' It was the Polish man who had taken my photo on the Pyrenees. I was pleased to see him and I was glad I could now put down this

WALK

uncooperative stick. After he took my photo, I joked that I would see him at the top for another photo.

I headed off again to ascend the next ridge. Up above me, spaced across the top of the highest ridge, was a long line of wind turbines. As I climbed higher, these enormous structures grew bigger and towered over me. They produced a constant whirring noise as the wind drove around their propellers. I had never been so close to them before, and I found them fascinating to watch in action and intimidating to walk beneath.

I was tired when I reached the summit of the mountain. The metal statues came into view as I rounded the last curve. The view of the valley from here was extensive, reaching out for miles. It was very windy. I wanted to take a photo but it was crowded with other pilgrims taking their photos. Instead, I sat down on a concrete ledge and pulled out a bocadilla I had purchased at the village before the last section of the climb. When my sandwich was finished, I walked towards the statues. A young Japanese pilgrim offered to take my photo. I handed her my phone and stepped into place between the pilgrims made from iron. She happily snapped me from lots of different angles just like any Instagram professional of her age.

It was a steep decline going down the other side of the mountain. There was little shade. It was dry, dusty, and extremely hot. Lots of loose rocks and stones made it dangerous. It was essential to stay focused to make sure each step was carefully placed. I felt like I was at my first skating lesson. The solid boots I was wearing made sure my feet were protected and my walking poles helped to stabilise me when I lost balance. I was absorbing the intensity of the heat and I must have drunk about three litres of water.

Pamplona to Puente La Reina

In Muruzabel, I saw a detour sign suggesting a visit to Eunate. This is a small Romanesque church built in an octagonal shape. Taking this detour would add almost three extra kilometres to my walk, but I was curious about this mysterious church. I thought that if I didn't go and see it, I would probably wish I had. To follow the detour, I had to turn left and walk off the main Camino path through the town. I passed by a bar and because my water was getting low I went in to get some more.

Sitting at the counter was another pilgrim waiting for his order. We shared light conversation as I stood beside him and patiently waited. The lady working there came back to the man with his order and then she turned to walk away. I caught her attention by saying excuse me and asked for a bottle of water. She did not understand me and kept pointing to the beer the pilgrim next to me had. She was irritated and cranky and she did nothing to cover up her annoyance with me. I finally remembered the word 'agua' for water and with a huff, she brought me back the smallest bottle of water I had seen. Not wanting to upset her anymore, I said 'gracias' and paid for it. I said goodbye to the other pilgrim and went on my way wondering what the lady would have done if I had been brave enough to ask her to bring me a second bottle.

The walk to the church was quite isolated. It was a farming area and there were capsicums growing. At first sight of the church, I wasn't very impressed and thought I might have wasted my time. But as I got closer, I could see the structure of the arches around the church and while it was small, it dominated the landscape from where it was positioned. There was a sign pointing towards a building beside the church advertising an entry fee. The young man at the ticket counter asked me where I was from. He was excited to hear that I lived near Brisbane. He told me his brother, who was a civil engineer, was working near Toowoomba and he said that he would be going to visit him at Christmas time. He asked me lots of questions about Brisbane before he handed over my ticket.

There was only one other pilgrim at the church. He was either very religious or wanted to fully experience the traditions of the church. He had taken off his shoes and was walking anti-clockwise on a stone embedded path around the church. I did not try this but I had read somewhere about the symbolic purpose of doing this. I went and sat inside. The most heavenly music was being played and I enjoyed listening to it. The other pilgrim came into the church and lay face down on the floor at the base of the altar.

After leaving the church I headed back to rejoin the Camino trail. Up ahead of me, a van was stopped in the middle of the path right where I had to walk. Two young men were standing beside the van. It seemed odd and I became concerned when I saw that the side door of the van was left open. Of course, I immediately started imagining that I was about to be abducted, but then reasoned with myself about why anyone would want to abduct a tired, middle-aged pilgrim. I kept walking towards the van while continuing to plan my escape. My plan to escape was not very clear because I couldn't have run with my backpack and I wasn't sure at what point I would drop it and then run. And then, if I could drop my backpack in time, I was so hot and tired and sore, that running would have been impossible anyway. In the end, I just decided that I would continue and take my chances. As it turned out, the two young men were setting up a drone and other than saying *'Buen Camino'*, they had no interest in me at all.

I followed a bitumen road back into a town called Obanos where I could rejoin the Camino path. There was an unavoidable steep hill to walk up and it was punishing. I thought that it wasn't very fair

Pamplona to Puente La Reina

given that I had already walked the extra distance to the church. As I got to the top of the hill and walked into the town, I saw three female pilgrims putting on their backpacks and readying themselves to start walking. I timed it perfectly and reached them before they left. I said hello and casually joined their group like I was one of them and they had just been waiting for me. They were setting a fairly robust pace as we walked and I joined in like I was a new carriage on the last train out of town. The only way I thought I would find the energy to keep going from here was to feed off their energy.

I learned that one of the ladies was from Cornwall and the other two from Northern Ireland. They were walking with small packs and told me that they were part of an organised tour and were having their big bags transported. Their accommodation was also organised through the tour group. The mention of Cornwall caught my attention and I said I had been watching the series *Poldark*. This series had a lot of meaning to me as I had been watching it with my dad in the time before he passed away. It hurt to keep up with these ladies but they unknowingly paced me into Puenta la Reina much quicker than I might have otherwise arrived. I said goodbye and wished them *'Beun Camino'* as my albergue accommodation was the first building we came to.

It was my first night in an albergue. I hadn't intended to stay in any albergues but I had managed to get a private room at this one. After sorting out my gear and showering, I went out to the garden area and bought a Coke. I needed something really cold with a hit of sugar. While I enjoyed my drink, I read the guide book to see what was ahead of me tomorrow. I was not eating a full dinner tonight. I had some snacks to eat and that would get me by until breakfast in the morning.

CHAPTER 6

PEUENTA LA REINA TO ESTELLA

DAY 5 – 22 KM

*'Enjoy the little things in life,
because one day
you may look back and realise they are the big things.'
Robert Brault*

I was awake early. My legs were very sore last night and the pain had caused a restless sleep. During the night, I had to get up and rub muscle cream into them. I was ready to go to breakfast at 6 am. I asked two pilgrims where breakfast could be found. They looked at me strangely as if I should know this information. I probably would have if I had eaten dinner last night. They pointed around the corner. I headed in that direction. I walked into the bar and handed over my breakfast voucher. I was brought toast and jam, a cafe con leche and a juice. I retreated to a booth and ate

WALK

my breakfast while I studied the other people in the bar. Some were locals and some were pilgrims. It was a great breakfast and feeling satisfied I left the dining room and went back to my room to finish packing.

It was still dark when I left my room at about 7:30 am. I was dressed in the pants I had washed last night. They were still damp at the bottom of the legs and as usual, I had a pair of socks pinned to my backpack.

I crossed over a long stone bridge and followed a wide section of the Arga river out of town. It was a cool morning. I was wearing a scarf and a T-shirt. I was cold but I had only been walking for 10 minutes so I was reluctant to stop and take my backpack off and get my jacket out because my backpack was sitting beautifully this morning. It felt like it had finally found its spot. I had the straps tight on my hips so they carried the weight rather than my shoulders. Maybe after all the daily adjusting, I had finally managed to get the straps right.

I left this morning thinking that it would be an easy day, but it wasn't long before I was ascending a very deceiving hill. It started okay but by the time I reached the top, I was puffing, my heart was racing and I was overheated. The deception was forgiven only after I had caught my breath, steadied my heart rate and stepped on to a reassuring flat path. In the distance, built high on a hill, I could see the medieval town of Cirauqui.

When I arrived, there was a bakery straight in front of me and I went in. I joined a little queue. The locals were getting their bread and newspaper and talking in Spanish to each other while they waited for their turn. I enjoyed listening to their fluent language and laughter, and imagined they were talking about the fresh

Peuenta La Reina to Estella

bread, the news, the weather and their plans for the day. When it was my turn, I asked for a ham and cheese roll which was heated and wrapped up for me. I held it in my hand, as I walked further up the very steeply winding narrow streets with many beautiful, intricately carved and coloured doors making artistic entries to homes.

I found myself on some very isolated roads after leaving Cirauqui and the heat was tiring. A mountain range, well in the distance caught my eyes and I hoped I didn't have to go that far. After climbing another steep, dusty hill, I arrived in a small town called Lorca and I sat on a bench to rest. After this last hill, my legs felt drained and were begging for mercy. I was sweaty and coated in dust. I took the time I needed to rest, drink water and gather some willpower to continue.

After a short while, a fellow pilgrim joined me and we walked together for a couple of kilometres. He asked if I was lonely. I was surprised at this question because I hadn't even considered that I should be feeling lonely since I left Roncesvalles. I said that I wasn't, in fact, it was the opposite and I was completely enjoying the solitude. Spending time on the road with no-one in front and no-one behind was great. It was an exhilarating feeling to know that I was the only human in that particular space at that very moment.

I was always busy looking around. I saw everything from the great big views to the tiny little beetles crossing the path in front of me. It seemed equally important that I had observed both. I also felt that when I was on my own, I was the only one in the whole world who saw or would ever see these particular wonders of nature. My highlight today had been the noisy chirping provided by a never-ending chorus of hidden crickets.

WALK

They successfully cut through the deafening sounds of silence across the landscape around me.

Today was very dusty and hot and most of the day was spent on dirt paths with a constant up and downhill pattern. The heat was pushing me way out of my comfort zone and I was not enjoying it. In the end, I somehow managed to get myself into a rhythm and I just ploughed through towards the end. My poles were clicking in an upbeat pattern that I maintained as best I could. I didn't dare to stop for fear that I wouldn't be able to start again.

The walk into Estella seemed to take forever. The path took me in what I considered to be a very roundabout way to the heart of the city. I walked past sunflower paddocks where the sunflowers were black and bent over and dying. I felt like one of those sunflowers; dried out and wilting.

My hotel was in the main plaza. My feet and legs were aching and I was glad to see that there was a lift to get me up to my room. I had a shower and did some organising and then went back downstairs to get something to eat. There was very little open at this time of the day. I managed to find a cafe but the kitchen was closed. There were pre-made tapas in the glass-covered counter and I asked for a couple of them to be wrapped so I could take them back to my room. I walked back to my hotel and ate my snack while I read my guide book in preparation for tomorrow. I completed my organising for an early departure and went to bed.

CHAPTER 7

ESTELLA TO LOS ARCOS

DAY 6 – 21 KM

'Slow and steady wins the race.'
Aesop

Today, I was planning to leave early for two reasons. Firstly, I wanted to escape the heat of the day and the afternoon sun. Secondly, I wanted to stop at Bodegas Irache. This is a winery where pilgrims can stop and enjoy a free wine from the fountain taps outside the building.

I left my hotel at 6:30 am with the wine mission at the front of my mind but 40 minutes later I was still wandering around Estella, in the dark, looking for the Camino path. I was completely lost. The first lady who helped me took me to the bus station. Catching the bus to the next town would have been a great solution to my problem if I hadn't been in the middle of walking the Camino. The next lady who gave me directions worked at the bus station.

WALK

She sent me off in another direction and I ended up right back at the bus station.

The next person to help me was a lady waiting to catch the bus. This time I was ushered away from the bus station in the opposite direction to the previous time. I had my map out in front of me, and because of a limited ability to read maps, I was manipulating the map like a Firewheel to try and make sense of it.

While I was studying the map (at least holding it the right way up), a car stopped and a man got out and came over to me. I was in a dimly lit area on the footpath so I was alert and cautious. Based on my map spinning, it would have been a reasonable assumption that I was lost. He spoke in Spanish and I simply said 'Camino'. He pointed me back in the direction from which I had come. I headed off with newfound confidence as this was the way that I had headed the first time.

I crossed over a bridge and walked into a very dark park. I was now becoming increasingly concerned. Any sense of direction I might have had was completely gone. I was scanning backward and forwards to find a way out of the park. I could see street lights and headed towards them just to get myself out of there. When I got back to the edge of the park, I saw another lady walking along the footpath towards me. Perhaps she was heading to work. I interrupted her and asked for the way to the Camino. She pointed in a new and different direction and my heart sank as I had failed to follow the directions of the last three people who had pointed. To my absolute relief, she then said, 'Follow me. I am going that way.' I must have said thank you several times. She led me through a couple of laneways and as we turned into a street she pointed for me to cross the road.

Estella to Los Arcos

There were other pilgrims on this street so I was finally confidant I was where I should be. The position of this street led me to think that maybe if I had just kept walking straight ahead when I left my accommodation instead of following the first lady who offered to help, I might have been here almost an hour ago.

I crossed the road and headed up a very steep hill. I was walking at a steady pace to catch up on time lost when I heard a whistle from the other side of the street. I turned to look and a pilgrim was waving at me and pointing to the right. I had been about to go to the left. OMG. Was there no end to this craziness? I had to do better than this. I had no sense of direction and the question was obvious, 'Should I even be walking across Spain on my own?'

I was soon safely following yellow arrows again. I came up to a young female pilgrim as we both searched for the next arrow. We found it together and started walking again. Her name was Polly. She was 18 and from the UK. She had just completed high school and wasn't sure what she wanted to do so she had decided to walk the Camino on her own. We walked together for about an hour talking the whole time. She told me that her dad had walked the Camino about 10 years earlier. I imagined her parents must be worried about her.

We reached the Monastery and the wine fountain. There were two taps: one was for water and one was for wine. I had saved a little plastic water bottle for this special occasion and I filled it with red wine. I had a bottle clip on the front strap of my backpack and I placed my wine bottle in here for easy access as I walked. I enjoyed taking little sips as I walked along. The wine was delicious, and I started to think that this might be an enjoyable way to start each day instead of a boring old coffee.

It was 10 am when we walked into a small village. Polly and I said our goodbyes. I wanted to stop for a while and have something to eat. The church bells were ringing as I walked through the narrow street. It occurred to me that on most days, I leave a town to the sound of a rooster crow and I arrive at another town, to the sound of church bells.

Estella to Los Arcos

My walk continued with a sense of peace. It was a warm day and there was a gentle breeze. The sky was spectacular. It was a beautiful deep blue with only a few clouds breaking up the colour. The hum of a tractor caught my attention as it ploughed up a field in the distance. Several eagles were soaring above the freshly turned fields. Everything just seemed to be in the right place today. Then, out of nowhere, tears started to form and flow. I knew they were tears of happiness because all these little moments had once again come together to create a priceless adventure.

It hadn't been a particularly challenging day, but my right knee was progressively hurting and slowing me down. By halfway through the day, it was giving me terrible grief and I found myself stopping often to stretch it out. As other pilgrims walked past me, they enquired as to whether I was okay. I assured them I was, but I was worried about it. I had no idea at what stage of the walk I had damaged my knee. During the last 3 kilometres, I had to be gentle with each step and it became a very slow walk. I was very tired and I hobbled into town today like an old lady, leaning on my poles more than ever.

It was siesta time when I arrived in Los Arcos which meant most of the shops and bars were shut. Luckily, I walked right past an open pharmacy. I went in and saw two different knee guards displayed. It took me much longer than it should have to overthink which knee guard would be best for me. When I finally made a decision, I took it over to the counter and paid and then sat on the chair in the pharmacy and wrapped it around my knee. I wasn't even sure that I had put it on properly. I didn't know how far I had to walk from here to my accommodation but at least I was going to get there a little bit easier.

I found my accommodation in an apartment building. I had a shower and washed my very dusty clothes. I then put my leg up on a pillow and rested my knee for an hour or so while I read my guide book for tomorrow. After my rest, I decided to head out of my room to have a look around town and get some dinner and some snacks for tomorrow. It was still siesta time when I went out

Estella to Los Arcos

and there was not much open. I went back to my room and did some basic organisation for tomorrow.

At about 7:30 pm, I tried again. I walked to the plaza and sat on a bench in front of the church and did some crowd watching. Restaurants were open now. I walked past a couple of them and there were lots of people enjoying lively conversations. I suddenly did not feel in the mood to eat in a restaurant. Instead, I went into a small grocery shop and bought a Coke and a packet of chips. I went back to my room and while I continued to rest my knee, I drank the Coke and ate half the chips. This was not a nutritious meal, but I was too tired to do anything else. I reflected on the daily highlights of meeting Polly, having red wine for breakfast and sipping it along the way, an incredible clear, blue sky, breathing in the fresh air and some tears of happiness. And with a happy heart, I rubbed muscle cream into my knee, feet and legs and went to sleep.

CHAPTER 8

LOS ARCOS TO LOGRONO

DAY 7 – 28 KM

*'Take each day as its own day,
and don't worry about it if you mess up one day.'
Henry Cloud*

It was 6:30 am and I was ready to go. After yesterday's messy departure, I managed to find my way out of town easily. Today was my partner Paul's birthday and I felt a little homesick that I wasn't there with him.

The first two hours of walking were in the dark. A spectacular sunrise emerged from this dark sky. A deep blue soaking through an orange base. The two colours merged to form a precious jewel in the sky. The view from the top of the hill was amazing because the sunrise stretched right across the horizon.

WALK

Other than the crunching sound of my boots on the gravel, it was a still, quiet morning. My knee guard was carefully wrapped around my knee and I felt like it was helping. There were many steep climbs and descents today and I was being particularly careful when going downhill as this seemed to be when my knee hurt the most.

On one particularly steep and rough descent, I had to be extremely cautious to make sure that I chose the right place to put down each foot. It was necessary to manoeuvre from one section to another to avoid areas where the ground had washed away and left a gap. There was no clear pattern and every step was a considered decision. As careful as I was to navigate the uneven ground and employ my poles to keep me steady and balanced, I still managed to lose my footing and slip. Thankfully, I landed on my backside with no damage to any part of my body.

At the bottom of this hill was a picnic area and I rested here for about half an hour. I sat on a small rock as I ate my snack. A couple came over near me and they were looking for something to sit on. I offered the older lady my rock. She declined but they sat together on the ground with me. They were a husband-and-wife team from Vancouver Island. He was 74 years old but did not look anywhere near it. He was obviously very fit and healthy. I am not sure how old his wife was but I guessed about the same age and she looked amazing too.

We fell quickly into conversation as they told me about all the walks they had completed. I asked if they had ever seen bears on any of these walks. They said they had. They told me that a bear is most dangerous when you surprise it or you get in between the mother and her cubs. They told me that one trick was to wear a bell. This warns the bears that you are coming. They said it was the cougars that were more dangerous as they would be more

Los Arcos to Logrono

likely to sneak up behind you. They have a saying, 'If you see a bear, you don't need to be the fastest runner; you just need to run faster than the person you are with.' I was glad there were no bears on the Camino because I was in no shape to run, so I would have been bear dinner for sure.

On the outskirts of Viana, a pilgrim from Taiwan started walking with me. Her name was Chin. We walked together for about half an hour before we reached the centre of town. We found it difficult to understand each other but we managed a stilted conversation about how we were each going on our solo walk. The main street of Viana was very busy as everyone was attending a beer festival. We stopped at a cafe and ordered some tapas. I ordered a creamy sausage and potato dish and teamed it with a beer because I was so dry and thirsty.

After lunch, Chin decided to go and over to the cathedral and see if she could get a pilgrim stamp. I had not been worrying too much about collecting stamps. I was just making sure I got at least one per day as required. I decided to continue walking, so we parted ways. I had about 10 kilometres to walk to Logrono which was where I would stay tonight.

I was just about out of Viana when I saw a cat walking towards me. It stood still, arched its back and started hissing. I thought it must be scared of me and if I kept walking it would surely attack me. I could hear a group of people just behind me so I stood still to wait for them. Suddenly, a dog ran past me. I let out a scream as the cat and the dog engaged in a scuffle. One of the men behind me ran to the dog and grabbed it by the collar and dragged it away from the cat. The group of pilgrims continued on their way with their dog, while I was still standing in the same spot, recovering from my fright.

WALK

It was very hot this afternoon and the sun was burning down. My shirt was saturated with sweat. My hands were dripping sweat as they gripped the top of my poles. I still had 6 kilometres to go to Logrono and I was feeling flattened by the heat.

Another kilometre further on, Beth and Jimmy who I had met on Day 1 at Orisson caught up with me. I hadn't seen them since that first day. We walked together for about 2 kilometres and chatted about a variety of things. The heat was exhausting me and I was getting tired and could not keep up with them. I bid them farewell and stopped for a break under a shady tree. They were concerned about going on and leaving me but I assured them I was alright and just needed a rest. They checked that I had plenty of water with me, which I did, as I had filled my water bladder in Viana.

I pushed on and made it to Logrono but as usual, my sense of direction was lacking and I could not locate my accommodation. I asked several people for help and they either could not understand me or did not know where my hotel was. One young man showed me a map on his phone. I went off in the direction he indicated but I was still lost. I tried to turn on my phone data to access a map but it would not connect. I had no choice but to keep looking but I was getting more exasperated and feeling helpless and for the first time on this walk, I felt like I might not be able to do this on my own. I saw a group of policemen walking through the mall and I asked them to help me. I showed them the name of my hotel and they happily escorted me through the streets to the hotel entry. I was appreciative and happy that I had asked them to help me.

It turns out that instead of taking the first bridge into Logrono, I had taken the second bridge. If I had taken the first bridge I would have found my accommodation easily as it was right at the end of that bridge. The accommodation I had booked tonight was

Los Arcos to Logrono

way too luxurious for the Camino and not required for my simple purposes of washing clothes and sleeping. I felt like I had wasted money and was now even more annoyed with myself. I was tired and I was feeling miserable and my resilience was lower than I thought possible. The early start today had not helped me avoid the burning sun in the later part of the afternoon and the walking time had been extended by an hour due to being unable to find my accommodation. The Camino had sucked out all traces of my positivity and optimism today and I felt defeated.

After showering and washing my clothes, I felt a little better. I went back out for a walk to check on the location of the Camino path so I would be able to find it tomorrow morning in the dark. I had to have a smooth departure in the morning if I was going to get back some positive vibes. I knew that I also had to do better with my navigation in the cities. Hoping to improve my mood, I treated myself to a mango gelati and walked back to my room. I wasn't interested in any further social interaction today.

CHAPTER 9

LOGRONO TO NAJERA

DAY 8 – 30 KM

*'You're only here for a short visit.
Don't hurry, don't worry.
And be sure to smell the flowers along the way.'*
Walter Hagen

It is 6:20 am and the streets are still full of people partying from the night before. Plastic cups are littered everywhere and the smell of alcohol and urine is intense. Logrono is recognised as the wine capital of this region, so I guess everyone was enjoying that wine last night and into the early hours of this morning. Just as I was thinking who might be going to clean up this mess, I notice a large group of council employees around the corner, busy at work cleaning the streets with shovels, brooms and high-powered hoses.

It was to be a 30 kilometre walk today with very little shade expected towards the end of the day. Leaving early would help me beat as much sun as I could. On the edge of town, I walked through a fairly big industrial area. I was a little spooked with not another person in sight. I was constantly scanning for Camino signs to guide me in the right direction. I could not entertain the thought of getting lost and doing even an extra 10 steps today after my day yesterday.

I was wearing my headlamp as usual. It was essential safety equipment for me because I left in the dark most mornings. Often, I was on a path or road with no street lights. If you are planning to walk the Camino but do not think you will do early morning starts, I would still suggest you bring a head lamp with you. Just in case.

My reality this morning was sombre and cheerless. I felt exhausted. I had bags under my eyes. My hair was messy. My shoulders were sore and bruised from my backpack. My feet were hurting and I now had two sore knees. It was my son Clinton's birthday too, so I was feeling a touch of homesickness for the second day in a row.

As I walked, the rhythmic crunch of my boots on the gravel brought my thoughts to reflect on my very difficult day yesterday. Yesterday played havoc with my physical and mental wellbeing and my resilience dived to an all-time low. This Camino walk is hard. Last night I pondered on questions such as, 'Why am I here?', 'Why am I putting myself through this?', 'Why am I always setting myself difficult challenges?', 'Why do I have to continually find ways to push myself to my limit?', 'Who do I think I am letting down when I don't strive to achieve?'

The answers were not entirely clear but I realised that there was no need to make life harder than it had to be. I resolved to try and make things easier and choose the less difficult option from now on whenever I needed to and not feel guilty about it. This meant on the Camino and at home.

Logrono to Najera

All this thinking and resolution did motivate me to take action last night. I decided that given the intense pain everywhere on my body and my growing exhaustion, that I should have my big backpack transported today. There is some pressure that to be a 'true' pilgrim you must carry your backpack from start to finish. Don't subscribe to this sentiment. Have your backpack transported when you need to have it transported. It is a great solution for days when you are sore and tired or for anyone who wants to experience the Camino walk but for some reason may not be able to carry a backpack.

Transporting my backpack was easy to organise through the hotel. I filled out an envelope tag, put 5 Euros in it, and attached it to my backpack. My backpack would be picked up by a transport company this morning and taken to the hotel I was staying at tonight.

I felt liberated to be free from my big backpack today. I was wearing my fold-out backpack instead. I was carrying only the essential items that I needed for the day. The only weight was my 'full to the brim' water bladder which I could easily fit inside the backpack and still have the drinking tube at the side. I was wearing my bum bag on my waist as usual to carry my valuables. I had rigged up two loops to attach my poles to my backpack by using some Velcro strips I had brought with me. My wide-brimmed hat was clipped on as well. It essentially felt like I was taking a rest day.

'That's it!' I told myself that after the Camino, I was done with pushing myself unnecessarily when there was an easier option. I was going to start enjoying some luxuries and stop making everything so hard.

The reservoir outside of Logrono was beautiful this morning. Day broke just as I came upon it. The water was peaceful and serene and looked like glass in the early morning light. Fish were jumping and ducks were floating. There was a choir of birds singing and plenty of little rabbits in the grass. I tried to photograph them but I was unable to get close enough before they hopped away. This connection with nature improved my mood and reset my outlook to optimism for a good day.

Today the walk was through the grape growing area and it was all about wine and grapes. The vines were covered with dark purple grapes. The smell of them was strong and the air was filled with the scent of wine for most of the day. While walking past one farm, a farmer called out to me. He was making gestures I couldn't understand. I wasn't sure if he was asking me for a cigarette or a kiss. Either way, whatever he was indicating, I said, 'No thank you' and walked just a little faster to get out of his sight.

The temperature was much higher than I had expected. It was about 26 degrees. The path was rough and dusty with areas that were very stony. There was little shade. I was wearing a long-sleeve lightweight SPF shirt and plenty of sunscreen. My big wide-brimmed hat kept the sun off my face.

As I was trudging uphill, along a rocky creek bed, a young Mexican man caught up to me and asked me if I would get his sleeves out of his backpack for him. He said he didn't want to take his backpack off and if I helped this would be easier. I said, 'I know exactly what you mean.' He laughed and said, 'Of course you know what I mean.' Once he had his sleeves on, we walked and talked for a little while about where we were from. We both commented on how tired we were in the heat. It was good to hear someone so physically fit say they were finding the day difficult too. It made me feel better about my progress. He was much younger and stronger than me and finally, he headed off at a much greater pace

Logrono to Najera

than I could manage. I tried to stay in the zone and grind out the last few kilometres. All I could think about was a relaxing shower.

I found my accommodation with ease. To my absolute relief, my backpack was waiting at the door for me. I had trusted the process and it had arrived as promised. The lovely old Spanish man at reception checked me in. He could not speak much English but we figured it out. Unfortunately, once again, there were flights of stairs to get to my room. It was a modest and very old-fashioned room with an old single, wooden bed and a duchess with a mirror. It was in complete contrast to my overindulgent room last night.

I did not often feel hungry at the end of the day but today I did. I was looking forward to a proper meal. The kitchen in the hostel was closed until 8 pm and I just couldn't wait that long. It was siesta time and not much was open. I did find a bar but they were not serving fresh food from the kitchen until later. They had some cold battered fish in the form of tapas so I settled on that and added a cold Coke. It wasn't what I had been thinking of but it would do. After eating my fish, I went for a walk to check out the path for tomorrow.

Overall today was good. It had been a joyless start because I was so sore and tired but not wearing my heavy backpack had helped by allowing my body time to recover from the work of the previous days. I felt like I was 'back on track'.

CHAPTER 10

NAJERA TO GRANON

DAY 9 – 28 KM

'It is the friends we meet along the way that help us appreciate the journey.'
Unknown

I left at 6:30 am and it was my first day 'off stage'. This means that I was not starting or finishing at the recommended towns in the guide book. Walking through the streets of a big city, in the morning darkness, always felt a bit scarier than when I left a village. I had developed a phobia for little white cars. I was not sure where it came from but when I would see one in the dark, I got a bit nervous. Weird I know. It was random and had no reason behind it.

I felt energetic and was able to keep up a fairly good pace. It was very dark but I wanted to avoid as much sun and heat as possible. The predicted temperature was 29 degrees. Walking in the cool morning air was much more preferable to me than in the hot, burning sun.

It was still dark when I came to a deviation in the path. I had no idea which way to go. I walked backward and forwards searching, but I couldn't locate a yellow arrow or sign anywhere. I could not see anyone in front of me to follow, so rather than go the wrong way, I decided to sit and wait for someone else to come along.

I had stopped at a cafe earlier and bought a bocadilla which I had planned to eat, later in the morning, for breakfast. I located a log to sit on and to fill in time, I started eating my sandwich while I waited. I was halfway through it when a group of pilgrims came by. They were lost too. As I watched on, they split up and with their torches searched for an arrow. There was some yelling as they communicated with each other. The arrow was located on the side of a farm shed further up the road. I packed up and followed them. This morning, the signs and arrows had been more difficult to find than on previous days.

It took me four hours to find my walking rhythm and I felt like I was moving at a snail's pace. There was a soft, warm, gentleness to the day and a nice cool breeze eased the warmth of the sun. I was surrounded by mountains. The sky was an incredible deep blue with very few clouds breaking up the colour. The roads were long, straight, gravelly and dusty. I could see a long way ahead and behind me. The patchwork of the grain fields was a mixture of brown and tan colours and they stretched across the landscape for miles. Huge haystacks were scattered across the paddocks.

It was quiet except for the occasional, but appropriate, interruption of tractors working in the distance. Eagles were soaring and little birds flying in and out of the grass on the side of the road. I barely

Najera to Granon

saw anyone else today. Only a handful of pilgrims shared the path with me and we didn't share any conversations. The walk was silent for most of the day making it feel like, except for me, it had been abandoned. Despite the crunch of my boots on the path, the silence shaped my peaceful and serene mood.

It was almost 11:30 am when I walked into the town of Santo Domingo. I walked past a couple of bars but planned to stop at one on the other side of the town. I needed a bathroom stop and I wanted to top up my water bladder. To my surprise and dismay, there were no bars or cafes on the other side of town. I was annoyed with myself because I should have stopped at the first one I saw. I decided to continue rather than go back. I had 7 kilometres to walk until Granon and while I wasn't sure if there were any cafes or bars ahead of me, I hoped that there was.

After a couple more kilometres of walking, I desperately needed that bathroom stop. I couldn't hold on any longer. As soon as I saw a couple of bushes clumped together up ahead, I made a plan. It would require some precision just in case there were other pilgrims close by. I checked that no-one was coming up behind me and that no-one could see me from the road. I quickly unclipped my backpack, dropped it on the ground and then ducked in under the trees. I pulled down my pants and straight away I felt a prickly plant on my bare bottom. I had no choice but to continue as time was precious. At any moment, a pilgrim might walk past me. Then, when I stood up to pull up my pants, I caught my boot in a vine and unceremoniously stumbled out of the bushes with my pants still unzipped. So much for trying not to draw attention to myself. Luckily for me, no pilgrims were coming my way.

I was now surrounded by paddocks of potatoes. I continued on my way, walking beside the highway and thankfully the direct sun was off my face. I stuck to the edge of the road to take advantage of the intermittent trees that provided some coverage. I checked my water, and if I was careful, I thought that I would have enough for the last 5 kilometres.

I started to feel the bruising on my shoulders and hips which was caused from my backpack. It was painful. I had started purging something from my backpack each night to lessen the load. It was usually something small but everything that was taken out reduced the weight I was carrying.

I loved wearing my long-sleeved shirt. It was very lightweight and dried quickly when washed. I could roll up the sleeves in the morning and roll them down during the day so they would almost cover my hands. It was helpful for days like today when the sun and I were not on friendly terms when walking in the direct sun for hours with very little shade to rest underneath. My long-sleeved shirt became an essential Camino item.

I arrived in Granon extremely hot and tired. Before locating my accommodation, I stopped at a bar beside the church and ordered a beer. The hostel in which I was staying tonight was a little further off the Camino path than I would have liked but it was cheap. I wasn't surprised that my room was on the second floor. I didn't like it but I was getting used to it. My room had two bedrooms with a double bed in one and a single bed in the other. The bathroom was clean and nicely renovated and there was plenty of fresh linen available.

When my Camino chores were done, I rang my daughter, Chelsea. I told her how exhausted I was and she reminded me that I should be eating healthy meals to make sure I was getting enough energy. She was right of course so taking her advice, I headed back to the

Najera to Granon

bar. While I was waiting for my order, an older pilgrim lady came up beside me. She introduced herself and I did the same. Her name was Marie and she was from New Zealand. She was 74 and walking the Camino on her own. It had been something she had wanted to do for a very long time so she had finally decided to cross it off her bucket list. She had been walking the easier parts that she felt she could manage and then over the harder parts, she caught a bus or taxi.

Marie invited me to join her and another pilgrim from Brazil, outside at their table. I readily accepted the offer and headed out with my pizza and red wine. While we were talking, three more ladies joined us. They were from Dublin. The ladies from Dublin had a 'Camino week' every year and had been doing this for eight years. They didn't walk the entire Camino but they were more like tourists as they chose a different section to explore each time for that week. They were friendly and happy. They had the most engaging accents and I loved listening to them. It was a lovely afternoon of conversation, laughter and sharing stories.

Before I headed back to my room, I wanted to buy some snacks to top up my snack stash. I walked up the street to the little grocery store. It had a sign that said it would open at 6 pm which was only 15 minutes away. I decided to wait, but 6 pm came and went and there was no sign of the grocery store opening. I was tired of waiting, so I left and went back to my accommodation thinking I would just get by until I found somewhere for breakfast.

When I got back to my room, I couldn't get my key to turn in the lock. I tried several times to make it work. Each time I used a slightly different technique in the hope that there was a trick to it. I went back downstairs and knocked on the door of the office. It was silent and there was no-one in the foyer to help me. I went

WALK

back upstairs and tried my key again but it still did not work. I returned downstairs with still no luck in finding anyone. I thought it was a long shot but I sent an email to the hostel address asking for help. They would probably not see the email until tomorrow. I was worried I would have to sleep on the floor, in the hallway, outside of my room.

I found a young man sitting in the dining hall. He only spoke Spanish so after a fair amount of hand gesturing and single words he finally got the message that I needed help. He tried knocking on the office door as I had, but there was no answer. I handed him my key and asked him to try the lock for me. We went back up the staircase and to both my relief and embarrassment it worked on his first try. I thanked him several times and quickly went into my room. I had been in my room for about 10 minutes when there was a knock at my door. It was a lady connected to the hostel. She had read my email and had come over to the property to help me. I apologised and said that someone downstairs had helped. She probably left thinking I was a bit strange.

That night, I slept in a rickety iron bed that made squeaking noises every time I moved. But the noise I was making, was drowned out by the renovation sounds next door that went well into the night. Despite all the noises, I went to sleep fairly easily.

CHAPTER 11

GRANON TO VILLAFRANCA MONTES DE OCA

DAY 10 – 29 KM

'Everything beautiful has its moment.'
Unknown

It was 6:20 am when I left in the morning and it seemed particularly dark. There was no-one else in the street. I was very tired and yawning my head off. My left foot felt like I had pulled a muscle underneath it and both my knees were feeling dodgy. I had put the brace on my left knee thinking it would help to support the dodgy foot. Despite the run of random injuries, I felt that my fitness was improving and I was becoming stronger. My backpack seemed to have joined my team and was working with me. It felt like it was sitting in the perfect spot and was strapped on well.

WALK

This morning, I left behind an extra pen and my buff, as I had not yet worn it. It wasn't much but every gram adds up.

Leaving this morning was a bit daunting and I was feeling a little vulnerable. My headlamp wasn't projecting enough light in front of me. There was nothing to do but remain brave and keep going. I was constantly scanning for yellow arrows. I could hear a dog barking and I hoped it was behind a fence. The light of my headlamp shone on a paddock full of dead sunflowers and in the dark, it looked like a scene from a scary movie. I regularly heard little rustles at the side of the path. It was probably mice, rabbits or birds. I came upon a little black and white kitten in the middle of the road. He was meowing and wanted to play. I stopped to give him some attention. I talked to him for a little while and then said goodbye and kept going.

I witnessed an amazing sunrise. It was yellow and purple and spread across the horizon. It looked like a modern, watercolour artwork. I passed more fields of dead sunflowers. The smell reminded me of when flowers are dying and they are left in the vase too long. Although their days of vibrant beauty were over, and they were not their usual optimistic, bright yellow colour, they were still a stunning sight. Beside one of these fields, a snake, about half a metre long, slid across the path. This was the second snake I had seen.

The wind had picked up and I pulled my visor down like blinkers, dropped my eyes to the ground and stepped up the pace. I was hungry and wanted to get to the next town as quickly as possible. I had previously decided that I would always stop at the first cafe for breakfast. I broke that rule today and I wish I hadn't. There were lots of villages but they did not have a cafe or it was not open. I hadn't replenished my snack stash yesterday so I was keen to find

Granon To Villafranca Montes de Oca

somewhere to eat. I would have eaten a nut off the ground or a piece of fruit off a tree if I could find it. I was starving.

An albergue with a cafe was a welcome sight. I ordered a cup of coffee and a ham and cheese bocadilla. I ate half of it while I tended to my feet. While I was massaging my foot, I discovered a lump underneath the arch. I didn't know much about the anatomy of my foot but I suspected that this was a symptom of muscle damage. I massaged it thoroughly with muscle cream and then put on more Vaseline, which was a staple in my foot care. It prevented my socks from rubbing and causing blisters. I hadn't developed a single blister so I was standing by this remedy. As I rested, I watched several pilgrims walk by. I thought to myself, that everyone on the Camino is likely to be in some kind of pain at some time. It might be obvious as a physical injury or it could be a concern of the mind or heart. The saying that 'You should walk a mile in someone else's shoes before you judge' is very real out here.

Belorado is a town full of stunning murals. When you leave the town, if you look back, you will see two beautiful murals, each one covering the side of a building. One is of an older woman and the other, a young girl. The impact of this artwork, for an unknown reason, provoked a momentary emotional reaction in me.

From here, it was overcast. This was great as it meant that I didn't have to walk the last 10 kilometres in the scorching sun. There was a series of hills to walk up and down so my poles were in use but it seemed that when I had my poles away I had to take them out and then when I had them out, I didn't need them. It was a bit like carrying an umbrella. When you have got it you don't need it, and when you don't have it, it rains.

WALK

I walked past a sign that said 554 kilometres to Santiago de Compostela. I was mindful of how blessed I was to be able to do this walk. I was incredibly fortunate to experience each beautiful and different day and all that it had to offer. Even though it wasn't easy, I counted my blessings every single step of the way.

Five kilometres out of Villafranca Montes de Oca, I sat on a bench beside a fountain in the small town of Villambistia and ate the last half of my bocadilla. A young female pilgrim from Denmark joined me and we started chatting. She told me that this was the first time she had travelled out of Denmark. She was enjoying walking the Camino as she was able to travel on her own and be independent but still connect with others along the way. She planned to finish in Burgos and fly home.

I refilled my water bladder from the fountain. I had read a story about this fountain. If you dipped your head in, it would cure you of tiredness. I didn't try it but I should have. I still had 5 kilometres left to walk and while I wanted to get to my accommodation as quickly as possible, I was being careful so that my foot wasn't damaged too much more.

My accommodation tonight was originally known as the Hospital de la Reina and was now converted to San Anton Hotel. It was filled with antique furniture and all sorts of trinkets and luxurious artefacts. The lady who booked me into my room asked me how the Camino was going. I said it was hard. And she replied, 'Just like life.' I agreed.

My room was on the second floor but there was a lift to take me there. The bed was covered with a pretty, floral bedspread and had floral and green cushions on it. There was polished, brown antique furniture, green curtains and a large purple vase with a

Granon To Villafranca Montes de Oca

very big bunch of dried flowers. The bathroom was renovated and modern. There were complimentary toiletries and plenty of fresh clean towels stacked up. I thought that I would be sleeping like a queen tonight in this gorgeous room. I couldn't wait to go and explore the rest of the hotel.

Dinner tonight was a pilgrim's menu. It was lasagne with salad, beef stew with some fries, and then a crème caramel for dessert. All of that was accompanied by a bottle of red wine. This was a big meal, but I was hungry and had been burning up many calories so I ate it all. I sat with a female pilgrim. Her name was Colleen. She was about 60 years old and from Canada. She had walked the full Camino before so this time she was just picking out her favourite parts to re-walk. While we were eating our meal, we talked about our experience so far, some of the people we had met and our lives at home. I enjoyed the company for dinner and the chance to debrief.

I was in bed by 8:30 pm but I could not sleep. My legs and feet were sore. I had some tablets for pain and then rubbed muscle cream in to each foot and leg and elevated them on the cushions. The lump in my left foot was still there and I massaged it for ages. I was sure that this was the muscle tightening up. The pain persisted until the painkillers and muscle cream did their work. My prediction of sleeping like a queen did not happen.

CHAPTER 12

VILLAFRANCA TO BURGOS

DAY 11 – 38 KM

*'With small steps
we can do almost anything we choose.'
Unknown*

When I left at 6 am it was cold, and it was the first day I had worn my fleece with my jacket. It would be a huge, huge day. I planned to walk 38 kilometres. I thought it might be too much but I would just take it slowly. Although it was 38 kilometres, it was a relatively easy walk and would not match the challenge of the first day over the Pyrenees. For this reason, and the fact that I was much fitter than when I started, I was confident I could do it.

It was a different landscape today with scrubby trees and rocky paths. I passed through a town called Atapuerca which has an archaeological site where evidence of the oldest recorded human ancestors have been found.

There was an option to take a small detour into a village or walk around it. I seemed to be the only one who took the detour. My reward was a couple of paddocks of beautiful fresh, yellow sunflowers. Just before entering the village, I desperately needed to take a bathroom stop. I had no choice but to find a secluded area beside one of the sunflower paddocks. I checked no-one was watching and quickly dropped my backpack. My skill in choosing bathroom spots came into question again. My dodgy knee was making it difficult to balance and I put my hand down and in precisely that spot was another prickly plant. I had to keep my hand where it was to remain balanced because I didn't want to fall over and risk someone seeing me roll onto the ground without my pants properly on me. The prickle was mild and after washing my hands, there were no lasting effects. After sorting myself out, I approached the town. I could see a church that had fallen and the bell tower was leaning to the side. This was an unusual sight because churches were important to a town and were always beautifully cared for.

The entry into Burgos was a challenge. It was a long, uninspiring walk and I was not only exhausted but my feet had become so painful that every step I took was now causing extreme pain. There were two options to enter the city. I decided to take the suggested alternate route. Even with the instructions in my guide book I was confused about where I should turn off. I stood and waited until a group of three pilgrims came along. I watched to see where they turned off and then followed them. I tried to keep up in case there was another turn but I couldn't do it with my sore feet fighting me at every step. This path went along the fence of the airfield. It was boring and there were no views.

Villafranca to Burgos

After the airfield, there were again two choices. I chose the one that went by the river. This path followed the river through a large overgrown park. There were limited arrows and for a long time, I felt like I was in the wrong place. I was apprehensive. The path weaved around and sometimes split into two and I was never sure that I was taking the right one.

Because I was following the river, I was fairly sure I was heading in the right direction. It became less overgrown as I got closer to the city and there were now more people around. I was walking slowly. My knee, my ankle and both feet were all hurting. I crossed a bridge and headed into the city. This time, after being lost when I arrived in Logrono, I had taken a photo of my accommodation and I kept showing it to people and they kept pointing me in the direction I had to continue walking. I located my hotel in a small laneway.

I checked in and found a very basic room. I showered and washed my hair. I put on my walking sandals to cushion my feet and headed to the World Heritage site of the Burgos Cathedral. I sat in the plaza watching all the people going up and down the stairs and decided not to go in. Instead, I went to a cafe and ordered a hamburger for dinner and a glass of red wine. I then found a pharmacy and bought a second knee brace which was a long overdue purchase.

On my way back to my room, I checked where the Camino path led out of town and while doing this I saw a bakery with amazing cakes and pastries. I bought a small cream cake to take back to my room for dessert. It had been an epic day of walking and I was exhausted. I now hoped for a good night's sleep.

CHAPTER 13

BURGOS TO HONTANAS

DAY 12 – 31 KM

*'At any given moment,
we have two options:
To step forward into growth
or to step back into safety.'*
Abraham Maslow

It takes nine days to cross the Meseta, and today was my first. Some pilgrims skip the Meseta, as it is a desert landscape described as hot, dry, boring and repetitive. This is Stage 2 of the Camino and is known as the Emotional Stage. I had just completed Stage 1, which is considered the Physical Stage and Stage 3 to come is the Spiritual Stage. I had certainly experienced the physical, and already had touched on the emotional. My Camino stages would likely merge into a mixture of all three, the whole way.

WALK

I had a very restless night last night. I had two single beds in my room and during the night I felt like something was biting me. I got out of that bed and got into the other bed where I was finally able to go to sleep. I discovered a few lumps on my back and some bites on my face this morning. They weren't there yesterday, so I was suspicious that they were bed bug bites.

I was wearing knee guards on both knees today. I had massaged both my knees and my left foot with muscle cream and also taken an anti-inflammatory tablet. I had my jacket on but I didn't think it was as cool as yesterday. I wanted to wear my gloves but I wasn't sure where I had put them.

The walk out of Burgos was much nicer than the walk in. The path took me behind the cathedral. The construction, the architecture, the art, and the sculpture of the large cathedrals is incredible, but more beautiful to me, are the small humble churches in villages.

Once again, I missed the Camino signs. An old man walking his dogs whistled to me and called me back. He pointed to a little stairway I should have gone down. I thanked him and changed my direction to get back on the right path. That was fortunate, as I have 31 kilometres ahead of me and didn't want to do any extra steps.

It was not long before I was lost again. When I retraced my steps back to find an arrow, I met a young pilgrim from South Korea, and between us, we managed to navigate our way out of Burgos. We walked into a beautiful early morning fog and the sunrise was all shades of blue and pink. I took a lot of photos. We walked together for about an hour before we parted ways when I stopped for breakfast at the first cafe I saw. After breakfast, I was not in a hurry to put my backpack on and continue. I was still tired from yesterday's very long walk, my knees and feet were sore, I

Burgos to Hontanas

hadn't slept well and my bites were irritating me. I recalled my conversation with the pilgrim from South Korea. She had said that she had been sick for the last couple of days. She said that at the end of the day she had started the practice of thanking her body for the service it gave her.

I have been taking my body for granted. No wonder it was tired and sore. I had not considered that it was the vehicle carrying me through not only this journey, but my whole life. My body had been working extremely hard for the last two weeks. My lesson today, was to thank my body for its service and treat it with the love and respect it deserves rather than an annoyance to deal with.

Today there were more tears. I stopped at a tiny church in Tardajos and sat quietly, listening to the most gorgeous and peaceful music I thought I had ever heard. There was a nun inside and she was giving blessings to pilgrims. She gave me a blessing and put a little gold medallion around my neck. I wasn't sure what part of this encounter had made me so emotional, but I was truly sobbing as I walked along the path. The tears were pouring down my face. I put it down to the fact that I was tired and sore, and someone had shown me some kindness.

Further along, I met up with two ladies from Colorado. They were in their 60s. We walked together at a snail's pace for about 5 kilometres. We talked the whole time. The ladies told me they had actually left with one of the lady's brothers, but he had become unwell in Burgos and decided to go home. He had insisted that they continue. We stopped for a snack and then I left them and walked ahead. I thought that I should try and speed up a little.

I came to the top of a hill and below me was the town of Hontanas. I thought it would make a great photo. I just finished taking the

WALK

photo and put my phone away, when my boots turned into roller skates and just like I was trying to walk on marbles, my feet went from underneath me. I landed like an upside-down turtle leaning a little to my right side. No-one was behind me to witness my embarrassment but it also meant that there was no-one to help me. I lay there for a bit to gather my thoughts, and I thought about how I was going to get up. I had the weight of my backpack under me and two dodgy knees that were going to make it difficult to stand up. My poles were packed inside my backpack so they were of no use. I decided the best way, was to roll onto my side, and then get on hands and knees and try to stand up from there. My knees made the manoeuvre difficult, and as I put my right hand down, a sharp pain ran across my wrist. Somehow, I managed to balance and get upright.

Once standing, I was able to do a thorough check of my body and stocktake the damage. I was covered in dust but there was no blood. My backpack had cushioned the impact of the landing in the dirt. My right thigh was sore as I had fallen heavily towards the right onto my GoPro which I carried in that pocket. My right wrist was sore as I had used my hand to break my fall. I didn't think it was broken. I did the best I could to dust myself off with my left hand, took a deep breath and went down the hill. Hontanas was just ahead, and I hobbled off, still trying to figure out how that impressive fall had happened. I was pleased when I got to the bottom and was still on my feet.

I bought a Coke and sat outside on the shop bench and drank it. As I skulled it down, I observed a couple of female pilgrims sitting on a bench on the other side of the footpath. One of them had her arm in a sling and was telling the story of her fall a couple of days earlier. I heard her say that she was going to the next town and then going home. I dared not think that this would be my story tomorrow.

Burgos to Hontanas

I stayed tonight at a brand new albergue. I had a private room. I joined the communal dinner with about 10 other pilgrims. Marie, who I had met in Granon, was there. It was great to see her again. It was the biggest group of pilgrims I had been with. Dinner was a delicious pilgrim's meal. It started with a salad. We then had a magnificent paella which came out to the table in the largest pan I had ever seen. The third course was a crème caramel for dessert. There was plenty of red wine and conversation. It was a Camino version of a campfire, with everyone sharing news, stories and adventures.

During this dinner, I learned that the cathedral at Santiago was shut for renovation. Last year when my daughter and I had walked from Astorga to Santiago, the outside of the cathedral was covered in scaffolding and was under renovation. We had been able to go inside and attend the Pilgrim Mass and we saw the Botafumerio swing. It was a lovely mass and we got to catch up with a couple of pilgrims we had met along the way. Now, it was the inside that was being renovated.

Some of the ladies staying here, including Marie, were taking taxis and buses throughout the Camino. This is a very difficult walk and pilgrims need to do what they have to do to get through it. There are lots of options to make it easier such as taxis, buses, bag transport and walking shorter distances each day. Parts of the Camino are much harder than others and it is sensible for people to consider what is safest for them. It's not cheating; it's smart. I applaud the pilgrims who make these decisions. Especially Marie. At 74 years of age, she has the courage to fulfil a lifelong dream. It is just different from how she would have done it at 30 or 50 years of age. The Camino takes courage no matter how you do it, especially when you are travelling solo.

WALK

'*Ultreia*' is a word you often hear and see on the Camino. It means to move forward with intention and courage. As long as a pilgrim is doing this every day, then they are travelling well. It is important to focus on your path and acknowledge that the path someone else is taking, is theirs to choose.

CHAPTER 14

HONTANAS TO BOADILLA DEL CAMINO

DAY 13 – 29 KM

'The journey changes you.'
Anthony Bourdain

After my fall yesterday, I decided to give myself an extra hour of sleep and casually prepare for the day. It was Day 2 of the Meseta and I had 29 kilometres to walk. It was a cold morning and I had thankfully found my gloves in my jacket pocket. I had them on, along with a scarf and my fleece. I had a whole lot of new injuries thanks to my fall yesterday. My knees were good but both were still braced. My wrist had extensive bruising and was too sore to move. I was unable to hold any weight with it so that made things a bit more difficult when I had my left hand only to pack and complete my morning chores. My thigh was bruised from landing on my GoPro and my chest and ribs were sore. I had

WALK

rubbed in plenty of muscle cream and had more than sufficient layers of Vaseline on my feet to stop the friction in my socks. My bed bug bites were becoming more and more itchy and irritating. It added a lot of time to my morning preparations since my body had been knocked around even more. But it was wise to ensure all creams and pain prevention were administered before leaving my room, so there was less chance I would have to do any running repairs on the trail.

This morning was one of my favourites of all. I could hear lots of field mice scurrying about completing their early morning business. Their burrows were in the banks of the path and I occasionally caught one in my headlamp because he wasn't quick enough to hide from me. There were a couple of rabbits scrambling to get out of my way too. It made me happy to see all these little creatures, and other than the minor noise they made and the crunch of my boots on the path, the countryside was silent. Despite all my injuries, I was feeling fit, happy and healthy, and looking forward to a great day.

As I walked into a small town and was admiring the ruins of a monastery, I noticed two very big dogs coming towards me. This was not one, but two of my worst nightmares. One of the dogs was a German Shepherd and the other I wasn't sure of the breed, but it was big. There was nowhere for me to retreat to. I looked behind me to see if there was something to stand on or hide behind and saw two male pilgrims approaching. I calculated that by the time the dogs arrived at me so would these two men. That is exactly what happened and when the men saw the dogs, they stopped and patted them. I stood to the side and watched. I mentioned I was scared of dogs, so while they were keeping them entertained, I quickly walked away.

Hontanas to Boadilla del Camino

One of the men caught up to me a little later and introduced himself as John. He was from Ireland. We fell easily into conversation and walked together for about a kilometre and a half to the next town. We stopped to eat breakfast. John's friend Pat met up with us at the cafe. Both men were in their early 60s and were walking for a couple of weeks to Leon and then flying back to Dublin. They were genuinely good company and I really enjoyed eating breakfast with them.

While we were having breakfast this morning, I told them about my fall. John said that I should have had my bag transported today and I told him I thought about it, but I decided that was the easy option. He said, 'If you had made that decision, it would have been a wonderful weight not only off your shoulders, but your mind and you would be walking with freedom.' This was not the first time and would not be the last that I would consider the theme of this comment during my walk.

Knowing that there was a big mountain crossing up ahead and the morning was warming up, I decided to get going. Thinking that John and Pat would surely catch up to me, I said, 'I will probably see you at the next hill.' Pat said, 'No you won't,' and I replied that I was very slow. Pat said, 'No. That is being pessimistic. We will never see you again.' I digested that thought and said with a smile, 'You're right. You will never see me again.' I made a mental note that from now on, I was going to speak more positively and avoid self-doubt about my ability to complete this walk. As I left, John called out to me and said, 'Remember, walk with freedom', referring to our conversation about the backpack.

The mountain of all mountains was coming up ahead of me. I could see it in the distance and the optimistic feeling I had gained at breakfast was growing dim. I kept walking towards the

WALK

mountain but while my body was going forward, my mind was resisting. Earlier this morning, I was thinking that if this was my office today, I was blessed, but now I had looked at this mountain climb waiting in my in-tray and I did not want to deal with it. Unfortunately, standing and staring at it was not going to help. I thought about a song I knew and quietly said the words. 'I can't go under it. I can't go around it. I have to go over it.' So off I went. One step at a time.

To my delight, I managed this mountain with more ease than I thought I would. I was fitter than I was 13 days ago. Thirteen days ago, this mountain would have taken me a long, long time to conquer. The view on the other side of the mountain was spectacular. The brown, yellow, gold and cream colours of the fields below blended and looked like a tub of vanilla ice cream with swirls of caramel.

After descending this mountain and walking for a number of kilometres, I went into a cafe to get out of the hot sun for a while. It reminded me very much of an outback pub in Australia. I was craving a Coke. I had started to drink one on most days. I ordered a sandwich as well. The bread was so crusty that I thought I would lose a tooth if I continued to bite into it. However, the ham and the cheese inside were tasty, so I took them out of the bread and ate them and left the crust on the plate.

John and Pat walked in and joined me. They looked exhausted. They had found the heat today a big challenge. Pat was in terrible pain with his feet. I passed on my tip of muscle cream. I also mentioned about rubbing Vaseline on my feet before I put on my socks. To my surprise, neither of them was aware of this. I had a new tube of muscle cream in my backpack, so I gave another half-full tube to Pat to keep. He was grateful. I finished my Coke,

Hontanas to Boadilla del Camino

bid them well, and headed off again. Just as I stood up, a pilgrim I had met at dinner last night came into the cafe. He gave me the hugest greeting like I was his closest friend. It felt nice that someone else knew my name and was happy to see me.

The last 6 kilometres were very tiring. It was a very hot day and these last kilometres dragged on. It felt like I was walking in a sauna. Despite the heat, today was a comfortable walk even with the many aches and pains I had accumulated. That big mountain I had wanted to avoid was a major accomplishment because 13 days ago, I would have struggled to cross over it. I was feeling pretty pleased with myself. My highlight today was without a doubt, meeting John and Pat from Ireland. Staying on my feet was up there with the top achievements as well.

CHAPTER 15

BOADILLA DEL CAMINO TO VILLALCAZAR

DAY 14 – 21 KM

*'It was when she walked alone that
she discovered her strength.
It's hard to walk alone …
But sometimes, that is the walk that makes you strongest.'
Muses from a Mystic*

I had done it again. I hadn't checked the Camino path out of town and so I spent a good 10 minutes wandering around looking for arrows. They can be so tricky to find and then when I do find them, they seem so obvious.

My legs felt good and were not sore. I had noticed that the bites on my face were quite red but they were not itchy. However, the bites on my hips where my backpack sat were very itchy.

WALK

I walked the entire 5 kilometres from Boadilla del Camino to Fromista in the dark. I could see the lights of villages in the distance and I could hear a rooster crowing and several dogs barking. I couldn't see much past the circle of light from my headlamp but I was aware that I was walking beside a canal for most of the way. I could hear the fish jumping and splashing into the water. The canal was on my right side and to the left, large trees lined the path. The wind was blowing the branches wildly and birds that were nesting in the trees flew out as I walked past. I wasn't sure what they were but they seemed large because I could hear the power in their wings as they flew.

While sight was always the key sense in the dark, it was a great time to get in tune with all the other senses. It was natural to constantly scan around to ensure that I didn't walk into things or trip over but it was an exhilarating feeling to be reliant on other senses as well. While I couldn't visually experience everything in the dark, there was still a sensory overload in other ways such as a cool breeze in my face, the fresh air that comes into my nose as I breathe in and the mist leaving my mouth as I breathe out. I heard rustling in the grass and there was always the sound of my footsteps as my boots crunched on the gravel in a steady rhythm on the path. This morning I was reminded of when I was a child and we visited the Bunya Mountains. Some nights, we would line up in a single row with only the first person in line holding a torch. We would follow along the rainforest walking paths, hanging on to the person in front, and trusting that they would keep you safe. It was scary but also fun. These morning walks in the dark felt like the same kind of adventure.

I stopped in Fromista for breakfast. I took my order and went outside to sit at the tables. I heard someone call out my name. It was Brad. I had met him two nights before at the communal

Boadilla del Camino to Villalcazar

dinner in the albergue. He waved for me to join him. I picked up my breakfast and went over to his table. We talked for about half an hour, while we finished breakfast. It was still dark and I wanted to make the most of the cool time in the morning before the heat, so I readied myself to leave. Brad said he would join me.

Brad would normally walk at a fast pace, but his foot was sore, so he slowed down and walked with me at my pace for about 3 kilometres. We spent that whole time in steady conversation. When we came up to a fork in the road, we parted ways. Brad went left with other pilgrims and I went right on my own. He said he hoped to see me in the next town so he would know that I had was not lost. I didn't see him again but I did speak to others who had met him. He was a big man and walked like a machine so it was no wonder that I never caught up with him again.

From the fork in the road, I followed an overgrown river path. I spent a good portion of the time wondering if I was heading the right way but I was learning to relax about this. I knew now that I just had to keep going and I would get somewhere. The worry of getting lost was lessening each day. Further along, I could see other pilgrims walking on the road adjacent to my path. It was overcast and felt like it might rain. It was still only 10 am and I was enjoying that I was not in the sun. I came out from the river path into a village. There was a little stone bridge to cross. I sat on the edge of the arch sides, and took off my boots and socks, and reapplied muscle cream and Vaseline. I was discovering the pleasure of slowing down and not feeling the pressure to rush through the day. I was spending more time talking to other pilgrims and to my introverted astonishment, I was enjoying making the connections.

The last part of today's walk followed a river. It was mostly dirt and grass which was always better than walking on bitumen.

WALK

The temperature was not high and that was making the walk comfortable. The scenery was not that different from yesterday, there was still lots of browns and golds. It was incredibly quiet; almost silent. There were lots of trees and I could hear the faint sound of water and occasionally birds. Running parallel to me on the other side of the paddock, I could see pilgrims walking along the road who had taken the same direction Brad had taken.

I arrived at my accommodation at about 11:30 am. This was unusually early in the day for me but I was looking forward to a restful afternoon. I would be able to take some time to pay some attention to my physical health. I showered and did my washing and hung it up in the window to ensure it absorbed a strong dose of sunlight. I had time to relax and give myself a facial using a mask satchel I had brought with me. I had not given any of them up when I decluttered my backpack. After my facial, I wandered around town and picked up some snacks for tomorrow. I located the path for tomorrow morning. I finished off in the plaza where I ordered a meal which would cover both lunch and dinner. A pilgrim sitting near me was writing in her diary. She closed her book and introduced herself. We shared some wine and chatted until we both agreed we were tired and left for our rooms.

I was learning to recognise and savour each moment that combined to make the whole day. These moments might include experiences with nature, interactions with pilgrims, physical issues, thoughts or times of solitude. They could be brief conversations or conversations that lasted for an hour or more. They all added unique value to my life because they were a part of the moment.

CHAPTER 16

VILLALCAZAR TO CALZADILLA

DAY 15 – 25 KM

'Slow down and enjoy life. It's not only the scenery you miss by going too fast – you also miss the sense of where you are going and why.'
Eddie Cantor

I intended to leave at 6 am but it was 7:15 am before I was organised. It was a night of broken sleep. I had a private room but the walls were paper thin and the man in the room next to me was snoring like a bear. I had put in my headphones and listened to some classical piano music to drown out the sound. Just about everyone on the Camino snores sometimes, whether they want to admit it or not, but you don't ever want to be the one who is awake and listening to someone else snoring.

WALK

Before I left, I adjusted the straps on my backpack again. It was a never-ending task, and I didn't know why I couldn't get it right. I was losing a lot of weight so maybe that was why the straps had to be regularly readjusted to fit me. My bed bug bites were irritating me this morning. I had three bites on my cheek, some on my arms and some on my back. The ones on my back were right where my backpack sat and were the worst.

It was a foggy morning and the sunrise was orange and pink with both colours flowing together. It was a long straight road out of town. I had started with gloves on this morning, but they were off now. My fleece and scarf were still on. I planned to get breakfast at Carion which was about 5 kilometres away. There was about 18 kilometres after Carion until the next town so a bathroom stop would at some time be essential. My water bladder was full, so I had plenty of water for another day with little shade.

As I walked through Carion there was not much open. It was Sunday and still early in the morning. I found a cafe and ordered a coffee and a bocadilla. I enjoyed the coffee here but kept the bocadilla for later. There was a service station just on the outskirts of town where I bought some more snacks for my bag stash, just in case.

I felt great this morning; fit and strong. My backpack with further adjustments was now fitting beautifully. There was still fog surrounding me. I noticed a pair of boots hanging in a tree. A wooden sign hanging beside them said *'Walk as if you are kissing the earth with your feet'*. That's what I tried to do today. I was slowing down and letting my feet do the work they needed to do. In return, I would take good care of them tonight. A Canadian man walked past me and surprised me when he said, 'It is a very boring today.' I did not agree. My eyes were constantly scanning

Villalcazar to Calzadilla

for new and different things. For me, today was not boring and not a single day had been boring. I sat on the edge of a culvert and ate my bocadilla. I attempted some selfie photos of my picnic. I was still awkward about this, and I was trying to do this while holding my sandwich. I set up my stand and held the remote. I waited for some pilgrims to pass and then took several photos while I juggled the sandwich and the remote. I was totally amused at my lack of skill and finally gave up trying to get a perfect photo.

In the middle of nowhere, was a pop-up bar selling drinks and other snacks. About 10 other pilgrims were taking a break. While I was giving my feet some attention, I heard a lot of shouting and excited chatter in the distance. It was a group of children approaching. There were about 30 children aged about 13 and five young adults with them. I assumed they were on a school trip. As they came into the rest area, pilgrims cleared out quickly.

WALK

What an extraordinary day it had become. The weather was beautiful. It was foggy but the sky was clear now and it was stunning. I could not take my eyes off it. The sky was my hero today. The beautiful shades of blue, the pattern and shape of the clouds and the horizon were picture perfect. I had taken many photos and I knew that no two would be the same. I was listening to some music and it had put a spring in my step. As I listened to each song, I dedicated it to someone it reminded me of.

The town where I was staying came up quickly. I checked into my room and did my jobs as quickly as I could. I went downstairs to the bar where I bought a beer and sat quietly on my own. I met a pilgrim from Finland a few nights ago and he said, 'If you can make it through the first four days you will make it to the end.' I was still doubting that until today, but after today, at the end of Day 15, I was confident I could. I went back to my room and as it was still about an hour until the kitchen opened for dinner, I decided to lie on the comfortable bed and have a little rest.

CHAPTER 17

CALZADILLA TO SAHAGUN

DAY 16 – 22 KM

*'Days are not for getting through.
They are for noticing, living and enjoying.'*
Unknown

Last night, although I planned to just have a little rest before dinner, I went straight to sleep and stayed asleep until the next morning. It was the best sleep, the best bed, and the quietest hostel that I had experienced. I woke up feeling great.

I had intended to have a coffee in the hostel before I left but I decided to get going and I would stop at the next town which was about 7 kilometres away. I put a banana in my pocket for when I needed a snack. I had given my feet the attention they deserved. Looking after my feet had turned into a ritual I performed every

WALK

morning and night. I was not just rubbing in muscle cream and Vaseline, but I was mindfully massaging them. The extra care I was taking was making a huge difference. As I left this morning, I thanked the owner of the hostel for such a comfortable room and a beautiful hostel to stay in. He blew me a kiss and wished me a *'Beun Camino.'*

I was walking along when a pilgrim caught up to me. His name was Peter and he was from Denmark. He was 60 years old. We walked together and chatted away. He told me that he had enjoyed his walk on the Portugal Camino so much that he had decided to come back and walk the Camino Frances. We stopped at a bar in Ledigos for a coffee.

Peter told me a story about one of his recent Camino adventures. A couple of days ago, he went out to a cafe for dinner and met some friends and stayed out much later than he had planned. At about 10:30 pm he went back to the albergue to find that he had been locked out. Some of the albergues have a curfew and if you are not inside on time, you are locked out. Peter rang the reception, but the lady who answered yelled at him in Spanish and hung up. He walked around the outside of the albergue hoping to find a way in, but could not find one.

Peter was worried because he only had a T-shirt, shorts and flip flops on and it was cold. He didn't know where he would sleep if he couldn't get in. He went back to the restaurant where he had been eating, and asked the staff if they could help. Two of the staff went back to the albergue with him. When they rang the reception, the lady yelled at them too. They walked around the building and found a bathroom window slightly ajar. One of the staff went back to his house and got a ladder. Peter scrambled up to the bathroom window and luckily managed to squeeze

Calzadilla to Sahagun

himself in. I am not sure how I would have handled this situation if it had been me.

Peter and I were both planning to go to Finisterre after Santiago so perhaps we would see each other again. I was almost halfway through my walk and I was starting to relax even more when meeting new people. I was finding it easier each day. In this way, the Camino was good for me, because I didn't have to join a group but I was still able to interact socially.

Over the last few days, I had stopped looking at the days as a mission to get through. I was letting each day roll out and at the end of the day, I was thankful that I had experienced it. I looked forward to each new day. I had learned that days are not for getting through, they are for noticing, enjoying and living. I hoped I would take this lesson home with me.

I stopped at an albergue cafe and bought a Coke and a packet of chips. There was a garden out the front and relaxing music was playing. Directly opposite where I was sitting was a church, where several coloured pigeons and just one white dove were resting on the edge of the bell tower. It was a peaceful moment.

As the day progressed, my feet felt like I had strapped bricks onto them. I trudged wearily into town like I did not want to be there. My hotel was close to the town entrance, so thankfully, I didn't need to invest too much energy into locating it. I followed my usual routine upon arrival. There was sun just outside the door of my room, so I laid my wet clothes over the chairs and railings to dry in the fresh air.

I went down to a pharmacy. I showed the pharmacist my bites and asked for something to help ease the itchiness and prevent me from scratching that part of my face off. By this stage, the bites on my face looked terrible. They were quite big and red. I was sure that they were bed bug bites from the questionable hotel I stayed in at Burgos. I desperately wanted to clear them up. I asked the pharmacist for some antihistamine tablets. Using his translation app, he said he did not want to give me anything chemical if I didn't need it because the cream he was giving me was just as good. I trusted him and bought the cream and hoped it would work.

I located a cafe for a snack. I was hungry and was craving pizza. Unfortunately, it was that time of the day when the kitchen was closed so I had to settle for a tuna salad, a couple of pieces of bread and a red wine. It was not enough food to satisfy my hunger and later that evening I ordered a pilgrim's meal in the hotel restaurant. I ate a big bowl of spaghetti, a thin piece of steak with salt, salted chips and a custard. I drank half a litre of water and had a couple of glasses of red wine. I left the dining room astounded by how much food I was eating now.

CHAPTER 18

SAHAGUN TO RELIEGOS

DAY 17 – 32 KM

'I came, I saw, I conquered.'
Julius Caesar

There was a cool breeze this morning. I was wearing my fleece but it was not cold enough for gloves. I had my walking poles folded and packed away knowing that when I stopped for coffee and breakfast, they would be out again because my knees were a bit dodgy and I needed support to get through the day without too much discomfort.

By the time I reached the outskirts of town, I was disoriented. I stood on the side of the road with my guide book and with the light of my headlamp I tried to work out where to go. I may not have learned how to navigate my departure, but I had learned not to panic. After taking a good look around, I was usually able to figure it out. The road to leave town was a dirt path beside the highway. The cars were flying past and it was very busy. I walked past a sign which said 315 kilometres to Santiago. That was pretty cool to see and I gave myself a literal pat on the back.

Today I felt like I had moved into a new tribe of pilgrims. I was not sure how I felt about not seeing the people I had already met. I had never intended to join a group but to my surprise, I did miss the familiar faces of the pilgrims who had crossed my path to this point.

Even after my big dinner last night, I was hungry this morning. I stopped at a cafe in the first town I came to for breakfast. I ordered a coffee and a donut. I was carrying a banana from yesterday so I ate that too. I was sitting at a table outside and a pilgrim came up to me and introduced herself as Trace. She said she had seen me walking a few days earlier and had noticed that I was wearing knee braces. She asked how my knees were and I said that some days were better than others. She said she had started to use knee braces as well. I told her that I had fallen over a few days ago and hurt my wrist as well and lifting my backpack onto my back had become a big challenge.

Trace told me that she was a Minister from California and asked if I would allow her to do a blessing. My sceptical attitude kicked in immediately but I said yes anyway. She held my hand and gave a blessing for my injuries including my wrist, knees and feet. It was a little like I imagined the practice of Reiki to be. I released my mind to the blessing. While I didn't believe that a blessing would heal my injuries, I was willing to accept that the power of positive thought might help.

Sahagun to Reliegos

Not far on from the cafe, I came to a crossroad. Most pilgrims had chosen to take the left option. It ran beside a highway and was four and a half kilometres shorter than the right option which was the one I chose. I had chosen this recommended route because it was supposed to lead me to walk on the finest example of a Roman road in Spain.

I was once again walking on a dusty road. At the sides of the road were small dense shrubs and bushes which were providing a limited amount of shade if I stuck right to the edge. There were plenty of flies buzzing around my face. It was quiet and isolated. I had resumed using my walking poles. They did make a difference in the stability of my knees. Seven kilometres later, I stopped at a cafe and ordered toast and coffee. I read my guide book and calculated that from this town it was almost another 18 kilometres of isolated walking. There would be no services and very little shade. That would explain why it was so quiet here. At least I had that Roman road to look forward to.

As I was massaging my feet, I noticed some backpacks sitting beside the reception counter. They were tagged and waiting for luggage transfer. I wondered if all these people knew something that I didn't know about what was ahead. Without hesitating, I asked the cafe manager for a transport tag for my backpack. I quickly transferred essential items to my fold-out backpack. I changed into my long sleeve shirt, filled my water bladder, put in some snacks, and made sure my big hat was clipped on. I thanked the cafe owner and set out to walk like a Roman on the finest example of a Roman road in Spain – for almost 18 kilometres. What was I thinking?

Thank goodness I made that quick decision to leave my backpack behind because today turned out to be harrowing. It was not the

WALK

most inspiring landscape to look at. There was nothing for miles. It was hard to locate any shade. When I did find a shady little tree, there were already three other people there. It wasn't long before another pilgrim joined us and there were now five of us huddled in this one spot and sharing a little patch of shade. One by one, like reluctant little chicks, each person took their turn to fly the nest and continue on the most unrewarding road so far on this Camino.

I needed a wee stop but out here on this Roman road there was limited privacy due to the barren landscape. As soon as I identified a potential spot, I checked for pilgrims. I decided that the opportunity was now. I swung into action and the mission was accomplished with my dignity preserved.

Later, I found another small tree to sit under and ate the piece of jam toast I was carrying. As I was sitting there a Dutch couple that I had met under the tree earlier, stopped for a brief chat and to check how I was going. The man asked if I was finding it lonely out here. I said no and that I was enjoying my time travelling on my own. He asked if I felt safe. I replied that I did. As he and his friend were leaving he said if you don't feel safe, scream and I will come running back. I thought that was very nice of him but I didn't really think there was any way someone would ever come back on this road. I finished my toast and followed along behind them.

It wasn't long after this stop, and about 2 kilometres from the end of today's walk, that I finally came to that famous Roman road. I had been looking out for it the whole way. Many parts of the road today had looked suspiciously like a Roman road to me, and I stayed optimistic that I was walking with the ghosts of Romans. When it was finally revealed, I couldn't believe what I saw. It was a very small section of fenced off stones which were barely visible

Sahagun to Reliegos

because it was overgrown with grass. I felt duped. I felt like I had been trekking for days across a desert to get a drink of water and the well was dry when I arrived.

Shortly after the Roman road, was the town of Reliegos. The Dutch couple had stopped for another rest so we walked into town together. The young man patted me on the back and said well done, you made it. He was either genuinely proud of me or was relieved that he didn't have to go back as part of the search party to find me lost and delirious.

I was exhausted and covered in dust when I got to my room. I found two single beds each with a pretty pink coverlet. I showered and washed my clothes and followed my usual post-walk routine. I went downstairs to the albergue bar and bought the biggest beer they had and also a large bottle of water. I went outside to the back garden and found a cool, shady spot to sit. I was joined there by Josh from Orange County and Sarah from New Zealand. Both were 29 years old and both of them had very sore feet. They could barely walk. It was reassuring to see that young people were having the same difficulties as me. It was easy to look at the young pilgrims and think they had it easy because they had youth on their side, but the Camino does not discriminate and injuries and challenges are shared evenly amongst all pilgrims.

Nathan and Jen, from New York, came out and joined us. It was their second time walking the Camino. They shared some hints and tips and after a couple of hours of sharing stories, we all went to our rooms for a rest before coming back down to dinner. It was a communal dinner of salad, spaghetti pasta, custard, wine and water. It was a fun dinner but we all chose to have an early night.

WALK

It was an epic day. I had chosen the recommended route so that I would experience walking with the ghosts of Romans past on the best example of a Roman road in Spain. It was a total of 32 kilometres today, with a quarter of them very remote and desolate, with very little shade available to rest from the burning sun. I was looking forward to a solid sleep after my Roman defeat today.

CHAPTER 19

RELIEGOS TO VIRGEN DEL CAMINO

DAY 18 – 31 KM

*'Patience is not the ability to wait,
but the ability to keep a good attitude while waiting.'
Joyce Meyer*

I woke up at about 5 am and was on my way an hour later. There was a chilly wind. The daily temperatures were getting lower each morning. Today's walk started on a flat, straight road so I could keep a steady pace. I knew that I wasn't missing much in the dark because most of the walking had been beside a major highway. By sunrise, I had already walked about 12 kilometres. I snacked on a few nuts along the way but as soon as I saw a cafe, I stopped and ordered a coffee and a panini. I set myself up in a booth and enjoyed my hot breakfast while I watched the flow of pilgrims and locals coming into the cafe.

WALK

Just after leaving, I joined up with a female pilgrim from Vancouver and we walked together for about an hour. Her name was Kerri and she was a retired park ranger. Kerri talked enthusiastically about how retirement had allowed her to walk the Camino. She would be spending two days in Leon and then bussing to Astorga. I was slowing down and stopped to rest while Kerri went on ahead.

The walk into Leon was like the walk into most of the big cities; long and tedious. I had heard that some pilgrims catch a bus from the outskirts to avoid the last few kilometres in the industrial areas. I had walked for about five and a half hours by now and my legs were fatiguing. The pain was travelling right up to my thighs. I took some time to sit on a ledge and rest. I had about 4 kilometres left to walk into the city. I crossed a big blue bridge over the highway and from here, I could see the spires of the cathedral. That was where I was headed.

Inside, the cathedral was stunning. The designs of the lead lighting were beautiful and the Gothic craftsmanship of the building was intricate. I thought Leon was one of the most beautiful of the cities I had walked through. I played tourist for about an hour and a half.

I continued on from Leon and when I arrived at my hostel today it was about 2:30 pm. The sign on the door said check-in was at 4 pm. I tried to open the door, but it was locked. I knocked but there didn't seem to be anyone inside. There was nothing else I could do so I sat down and took off my boots and socks. I leaned against a concrete wall and put my feet in the hot sun and gave them a massage. The warm sun was relaxing and I could feel myself dozing off.

At about 3 pm the door of the hostel burst open and the manager and her husband came out. They were horrified that I had been

Reliegos to Virgen del Camino

sitting there waiting when they had both been inside working the whole time. They checked me in and showed me my room. It was new, comfortable, and clean and had a comfy bed.

The manager could not have been more lovely. She made sure I knew where everything was and gave me a thorough tour of the place. There was a dining room downstairs and snacks available. I had wanted to walk further up the street to get some food but I decided against it given how sore my feet were.

For the first time, I did not wash my pants or socks tonight. My clothes were not too dusty today because today was mostly walking on the road. I just washed my shirt and underwear. It was nice to have the night off from washing.

I was really tired and every day ended in some kind of pain but I was still relishing my adventure and I was settled into the routine of the trek.

CHAPTER 20

VIRGEN DEL CAMINO TO VILLARES DE ORBIGO

DAY 19 – 31 KM

'Happiness is a long walk with a friend.'
cutehappyquotes.com

It was a bit cool this morning. As sunrise broke, the temperature dropped further. I had a fleece and gloves on.

Last night, my feet were cramping up. I had to massage them more than once with muscle cream. I was really worried that I was going to wake up this morning and my feet would be contorted into a twisted knot and would not unfold. The attention I had given them during the night must have helped because the cramping had stopped and the muscles had softened. I hoped they would

WALK

carry me through the 31 kilometre walk today. They had been working hard and I had never before thought about how much work my feet did every day to balance and carry me though life.

I stepped very gingerly out of the hostel this morning at 6 am. I was focused on my feet to make sure that I didn't step the wrong way and damage them in the first five minutes. I was feeling a few aches and pains right from the start.

The walk out of Virgen del Camino was not well marked and there were a few sections of road works to navigate. Because it was dark, I needed to be cautious and it took more time than anticipated.

Leaving in the morning darkness as a solo pilgrim requires courage and nerves of steel. You will be walking on an unknown path and your vision is limited. Sometimes you are walking through deserted streets. Sometimes you are on a main road or highway and at other times you are walking on a country path or a little path through woodland. Sometimes there will be a tunnel to walk through. Often, there are no other pilgrims near you that you can follow or walk with. You need to be alert to locate arrows and signs. For me, the use of a headlamp was essential. Most importantly, and this was a big one for me, if you do get lost, don't panic. Just retrace your steps and start again.

I was just 6 kilometres into the walk today and I was already hobbling along. The pain in my left foot was making it difficult to take a step. It was cold and I didn't want to take my boot off and rub in some more muscle cream. It was worrying me because as I hobbled along, I knew that each painful step was slowing me down and that meant that I would have to spend longer in the afternoon sun.

Virgen del Camino to Villares de Orbigo

I stopped at a cafe and bought a ham and cheese bocadilla and a bottle of orange juice. I took my food and continued to walk. As soon as it had warmed up, I found a place to stop. After I ate my breakfast, I took off my boots and gave my feet a long massage. I was worried about how long this would keep my feet in action, but there wasn't much else to do but pack up and keep going.

Josh, the young man I had met two nights ago in the albergue, caught up to me. We had stayed in the same town last night. He could see that I was having trouble walking and that I was reduced to a fairly slow pace. Several times I said to Josh that he should not wait with me, and he should go on. He said he was happy to walk slowly today as his feet were sore as well. We stopped at a cafe for lunch. I still had half of my bocadilla to eat. Josh went in and got his lunch and brought out a coffee for me.

What did we talk about? We talked about everything. Of course, we discussed pilgrim problems such as sore feet, accommodation and food. We talked about the colonisation of America and the history of the first Ten Amendments to the constitution. I had no idea about either of these topics and I was fascinated by what Josh was telling me. We discussed the difference between American and Australian laws. We talked about our families and we talked about our work. It was about 25 kilometres worth of conversation and lots of stories were shared. It was the first day I had walked most of the day with the same person.

I told Josh that when people asked me why I wanted to walk the Camino, I likened it to Forrest Gump saying, 'That day, for no particular reason, I decided to go for a little run.' I told him that I would probably get to the end and I would be just like Forrest again when he stopped running and he said he was tired and he was going home. How prophetic I was.

WALK

We walked together for most of the day. We talked non-stop all the way to the town of Hospital so time passed quickly. When we got to the town, we parted ways. Josh was staying here tonight and I continued to the next town where I had booked a private albergue room.

I had about 2 kilometres left to walk. As I came up to the first intersection out of town, a pilgrim was sitting on a bench flicking through his guidebook. I stopped and said hello and we briefly discussed which way we were going. He was heading in a different direction to me. I had seen this man a few times along the way but we had not yet spoken. He told me he was from Israel. He said he was struggling with the heat so he had tried to slow down and was departing for his days walk in the late afternoons to avoid the midday heat.

I said goodbye and plodded off on my own. I came on to a dusty, rocky road. I was probably walking about 2 kilometres an hour and I felt like I was dragging my feet. The muscles in my feet were screaming out and I was about as miserable as I could be. The Camino path took me straight to my albergue and I was welcomed by a lovely lady. She told me I was the only one staying tonight so she had upgraded me to a better room. It was a beautiful place. There was a fountain in the middle of the indoor courtyard and an uninterested cat who was a permanent resident.

My room was cosy and had a little wrought-iron balcony. There were two single beds and a modern bathroom. I showered and then went back downstairs to wash my clothes in the laundry. I hung them on a rack to dry in some patches of sunlight.

I went for a walk to find the supermarket. The streets were deserted. I seemed to be the only one in town. I found the supermarket and

Virgen del Camino to Villares de Orbigo

bought some dinner items. There were a few places where I could get some food later but I didn't want to wait until then. My feet were sore so I just wanted to stay in and rest.

CHAPTER 21

VILLARES DE ORBIGO TO ASTORGA

DAY 20 – 15 KM

*'Travel isn't always pretty,
it isn't always comfortable.
Sometimes it hurts.
It even breaks your heart.'*
Anthony Bourdain

My bed was comfortable, and I had a great sleep. I had put the heating on in the room to keep warm. Since I was the only one staying in the albergue, it was very quiet. When I had a shower, I noticed that the bites on my face were still quite red and raised. I speculated what other people might have been thinking when they saw them. Once I was semi packed to leave, I headed down to the kitchen for breakfast. I had heard the resident cat meowing outside my door and when I opened it, the cat jumped

WALK

up at me. I screamed and jumped backward and the cat ran the other way. I don't know which one of us got the greatest fright. My heart was pounding and when I had recomposed myself, I headed down to breakfast.

The lady who had checked me in had prepared a delicious breakfast spread which was set out in the kitchen like a buffet. There was cereal, fruit, juices, toast, yoghurt, breakfast biscuits, jams, honey and pastries. It was all just for me. There was way more food than I could eat. I made some toast with jam and bit into it. As I did this, a piece of filling broke off. This could develop into a really bad situation. There seemed to be no pain so I decided to keep the area as clean as possible and hope that I finished the Camino without a tooth crisis. I preferred to wait until I got home to get my tooth fixed.

I went back up to my room and packed up. I left at 7:30 am. I was heading to Astorga today. It was a short 15 kilometre walk. It was dark and there was a cold wind and I could feel the chill coming through my fleece. I was glad that I had my gloves. I was on the lookout for yellow arrows. I hesitated when I found one because I felt like it wasn't pointing the way I thought I should be going. I decided to backtrack a little bit to find previous arrows. I refollowed the arrows back to where I was and decided it must be the right way. My sudden confidence in being an authority on knowing the right direction, given my previous missions to leave towns, is something that did not go unnoticed.

Just as the sky started to lighten, I walked into a small town. This was my favourite time of day. I could hear a rooster crowing and all the little birds chirping. It was rare to see any locals up this early but there were a couple who appeared to be going off to work.

Villares de Orbigo to Astorga

Leaving this town, I had to walk through the middle of a dairy farm. I heard the sounds of the animals and could see a farmer working in the milking shed. I could smell hay and cow manure. I stopped and watched the little calves eating their share of hay. I turned around and looked behind me. There was a globe of beautiful orange rising above the mountains. The sun was perfectly round and the array of bright yellow and orange colours around it was brilliant. It was a spectacular event to witness. The sun was now lighting up the road ahead of me and was bathing it in golden light. I felt whimsical and started singing to myself, 'Follow the yellow brick road'.

It was only about 10 am and I still had 10 kilometres to go to Astorga. I had walked only 5 kilometres in three hours due to the pain in my feet. Every step so far had been like walking on nails. This was a sign that I needed to do some serious renovations on my feet. They were in shocking pain. I found a dirt mound and sat down. I took my boots and socks off and massaged both my feet with muscle cream. I also took a painkiller. I sat for a while with my boots off and kept up the massaging.

As I was sitting there, a couple of other pilgrims walked past me and we said hello. I snacked on a couple of nuts and had a drink of water. Peter came past and he stopped and chatted with me for about 10 minutes. I thought he would have been way ahead of me, but he was having some shin issues which had slowed him down.

When Peter left, I put my socks back on, and rather than my boots, I put on my trekking sandals. I thought that maybe the arch of the sandals would support my feet and make it a little easier to walk. I packed my boots into my backpack. It was not the most attractive look but at this point, I didn't care. I hoped that between

WALK

the muscle cream, the painkiller, and the sandals I would be able to continue to walk the next 10 kilometres.

Today was officially the last day of the Meseta. There was a lot of big trees and the path became more undulating as I got closer to Astorga. I used my walking poles to take the pressure off my feet. From the top of the final hill before Astorga, I could look over the whole city. I saw the cathedral spires in the distance. I looked towards the mountains and I could see that there was no snow on them.

Standing there and looking at this view, brought back memories of last year when I had walked the Camino with my daughter, Chelsea. We had started our walk to Santiago from Astorga. I was emotional because the walk we did had some very special memories. We had walked during March and April and we had to walk in the snow on some of those days. It had taken me three weeks to get back here to our starting point. I would experience the rest of this walk in a different way to last time because the weather was different and I was on my own this time. Love you, Chelsea x

The walking sandals had helped to relieve the pain in my feet a little bit but I still limped into Astorga. I was now in extreme pain. Every step I took was excruciating. I think now, I must have been walking at about 1 kilometre an hour. I couldn't do any more than that. I was weary, sore and emotional. Right now, I could have just laid down on the ground and given up walking anywhere. I kept looking up ahead of me at the cathedral spires. I was getting closer and I kept reminding myself I could do this.

To keep me distracted from my pain, I made a mental note of some things I needed to do when I got into the city. They included

Villares de Orbigo to Astorga

getting some insoles for my shoes, buying some chocolate, decluttering my backpack, and finding a post office to forward some items on to Santiago where I would collect them in a couple of weeks. Astorga was famous for its chocolate and since my daughter and I had not tried any last time, I wanted to get some to take home. It would be the first and only purchase I made on the Camino that I was to take home, until I reached Santiago. The chocolate was to be forwarded to Santiago with the other items. I definitely was not going to carry it.

It was a steep uphill climb through the streets into the centre of Astorga. I was not thrilled to see the extra steep hills I now had to walk up. I was asking myself why I would have thought it was a good idea to put myself through the experience of more than a month of solo walking. With this depressing thought, I pretty much huffed and puffed my way up these hills to find my hotel.

My hotel was in a large plaza and was quite flashy. I reassured myself that I deserved this luxury today. After checking in and getting myself organised, I went out to the plaza to look around. I had packed a parcel of items to take to the post office. I stopped at a chocolate shop first to buy chocolate which I wanted to add to the parcel. The lady working in the chocolate shop was rather rude and I felt that it was unnecessary and couldn't she see I had very sore feet and had just had a very difficult day? It was difficult to smile and thank her, but I did.

I found a *'Correos'* (Post Office). It was busy and I wasn't sure how the system worked. I waited in line and when I it was my turn at the counter, it turned out to be an easy process. I simply showed the lady at the counter the address of the Santiago post office in my guide book and she took over and organised everything. The post office in Santiago would hold the parcel and I could collect it in a couple of weeks. I headed back to the plaza and went to the pharmacy where I bought some insoles for my boots. The supermarket was next. I stocked up on fruit and snacks. With all my jobs accomplished, I walked up to the cathedral to take a look. I sat for a while on the bench and just watched the comings and goings of everyone around me.

Next on the list was my dinner. I walked back to the restaurant outside my hotel and went in and ordered a pilgrim's meal. I located an empty table outside. A whole bottle of red wine was opened just for me and placed on the table. The first course was pasta with Bolognese sauce and the second course was chicken and fries. I told the lady not to worry about bringing the dessert. I was ready to go back to my room and settle down for the night. I was satisfied with having completed my list of jobs and I was particularly pleased that I had bought insoles and sent my parcel to Santiago.

CHAPTER 22

ASTORGA TO FONCEBADON

DAY 21 – 26 KM

*'The mountains that you are carrying,
you were only supposed to climb.'*
Najwa Zebian

The bedroom was soundproof, so I slept well. It was 5 am when I woke up, and I knew that I was not going to be able to go back to sleep so I figured I may as well have a hot shower, pack up and get going. It was 6 am when I left my room and the bells in the cathedral were ringing as I walked out of Astorga. Today is the first day of Stage 3 of the Camino which is known as the Spiritual Stage. I had certainly experienced both the physical and emotional part of Stages 1 and 2.

Today I was planning to walk to Foncebadon. My feet were not perfect but they felt better than yesterday. I had put the insoles inside my boots and they fit well, and they did seem to be relieving the pressure on my feet.

About 5 kilometres out of Astorga, I came upon a female pilgrim who was rushing back and forth because she couldn't find which way to go. It was still dark and she just seemed to be walking in circles. She was very anxious. There were roadworks here, so it was hard to follow where the path went. I had seen an arrow earlier and I had walked this path on Day 1 with my daughter last year, so I was fairly sure where to go. I pointed to where I thought the path went but the lady hesitated to follow my advice.

She told me that she hated getting lost so she had two guide books with her and two phone apps. I said it is just a roadblock and you will just need to find your way around it. We navigated our way around the fenced-off part of the path when suddenly she thought it was a promising idea to take a shortcut through a ditch. Without thinking, I stupidly followed. Now, I had to get back up the other side of the ditch. I lost my balance in the sandy dirt as I tried to get a foot holding and I automatically put down my hand to balance. It was my right hand and my wrist sent out a sharp pain. I had forgotten it was still sore from my fall. I could not believe that this was happening. I composed myself and then took my time and scrambled out of the ditch in a fairly unceremonious manner. The other pilgrim was long gone. She hadn't even waited to check I was okay.

She was a curious pilgrim. I had seen her a few times before as she had hustled past me. Strangely, two or three hours later she would hustle past me again. I wasn't sure how she always managed to be so far behind me. She was very anxious each time I saw her but, she was walking solo, so all credit to her for meeting the challenge.

Astorga to Foncebadon

Later in the morning, a man in a yellow hoodie walked past me. He said, '*Buen Camino*' and I turned to look at him as I replied with '*Buen Camino*'. I took a double-take as I could have sworn it was Leonardo Di Caprio. It was unlikely but it might have been. Imagine that. It gave me something to think about for a while as I watched him go on ahead of me.

Today I felt like there was a huge wave of pilgrims going over me. They were rushing by with a sense of urgency. The dust was churned up with the stampede of boots and walking poles. It was freaking me out and making me feel uncomfortable. I slowed down to let the wave pass to avoid this frantic human tide. The reason that there was an increase of pilgrims this morning may have been that Astorga is a popular place to start the Camino. It is also where other Camino paths merge.

The sense of urgency was unsettling and to avoid getting caught up in the panic, I did the opposite and slowed down. I didn't care if I was last to arrive anywhere today. We were all heading in the same direction. The first and fastest had no value for me. I stopped on two separate occasions for coffee and then followed on behind. I was feeling much more relaxed. My mantra for today was, 'My path: My way'. My new boot insoles seemed to be working just as I needed. I stopped at a rest area and took the time to give my feet a massage.

When I stopped at a cafe at Rabanal, I bought a Coke to drink before I tackled the mountain climb up to Foncebadon. I took off my backpack and put it down beside an empty table. As I did so, a lady came out and said quite rudely that she had been sitting there. Her manner indicated that I should not sit down. I was surprised and trying to mask my shock, I bit my tongue and didn't reply. I picked up my backpack to move. She then told me

WALK

it was okay and I could sit with her. I politely said, 'No thank you. I will find another table.' In 21 days of walking on the Camino, she was the first person I had encountered to behave like this. This was very unusual because, pilgrims generally welcome the company of others, especially if they are on their own.

I found another table and drank my Coke. I wasn't looking forward to the climb ahead of me. It would be a difficult way to end the day. The wind was cold and tearing through the trees and the climb was even more difficult than I remembered. I worked hard to traverse the incline and the rocky ground. It was far from easy.

Astorga to Foncebadon

Chelsea and I had walked up this hill when we walked from Rabanal to Ponferrada. We had tackled it on our Day 2, in the dark and the snow. I made sure to let her know how remarkable she had been on that very dark, snowy, cold morning just over a year ago.

Foncebadon is a small village with many of its stone buildings in ruins. I checked in to my hostel and was provided a lovely little room. I had a pilgrim's dinner of delicious, creamy pumpkin soup, pork loin and fries, and custard for dessert. I did my best to drink the jug of wine that came with my meal. While I was eating, an American female pilgrim came over and introduced herself. Her name was Carol and I invited her to sit with me. She was from San Francisco. She told me that she had caught a taxi to Foncebadon yesterday while her husband walked as she had been feeling unwell. Carol's husband Jeremy joined us later and they ate their meal with me. It was lovely company to complete the day.

CHAPTER 23

FONCEBADON TO PONFERRADA

DAY 22 – 27 KM

*'This day is unique. I am looking forward to what I will see, who I will speak to, and how I will feel.
The combination of these moments will never occur again in the pattern they are about to today.'*
Unknown

The wind was howling, and the rain was whipping against my bedroom window. My plan today was to walk to Ponferrada but my first stop would be at Cruz Ferro. Cruz Ferro is almost the highest point on the Camino Frances. There is an iron cross on the top of a tall timber pole. Pilgrims traditionally leave a symbol at this cross. Often it is a rock they have carried from home, or something else, that represents a burden they are carrying. The symbol is placed at the bottom of the cross to represent closure or letting go of the burden. I sensed that it would be a significant day today for two reasons.

I had been through a very difficult and sad time in the couple of years prior to my Camino walk last year. I wanted to give closure to that time of my life. On that occasion, I had brought a rock with me that was taken from that place of sadness. I underestimated the power of the emotions I was still carrying and when I placed that rock down, all those emotions surprised me by resurfacing. I was overcome with tears and memories. I was grateful to have my beautiful daughter there to hug me that day. Even as I write this, I am teary and emotional remembering the occasion.

This Camino, I planned to place a symbol of celebration to acknowledge the wonderful life I have and the people who make it so special. I had brought a rose quartz crystal with me. This was a significant item because it was a crystal I had given my partner when he was going through a tough time. When we were discussing what I could take with me to represent my gratitude, he returned the crystal to me. I immediately thought that if I left this pretty crystal behind someone else might take it. My partner said if that happens it is okay. They must need it, and hopefully, all the gratitude that we feel will be theirs to take home.

The second reason was that just before I left home this time, another event had occurred. I have four sisters and we had always had a close relationship. A family event created a breakdown in this relationship and a division had occurred. At the time, I found myself in the middle of the division and despite my efforts to repair relationships, it had not happened. I was thinking about this on Day 1 when I walked over the Pyrenees so, I picked up a stone to represent this sisterly bond and I planned to leave it at Cruz Ferro as an affirmation that this relationship would heal.

Foncebadon to Ponferrada

I packed and went down to the dining area for breakfast. I had a leisurely breakfast with the American couple. We talked about our plans for the day. Today would be an uphill walk of about 2 kilometres to Cruz Ferro from Foncebadon. From the top of the mountain range, there was a steep and rocky descent back down on the other side. Carol said she was still feeling unwell and wasn't sure if she would walk today or get a taxi.

I was feeling patient this morning. It was bitterly cold, windy and raining outside. Because of my plan to arrive at the cross just on sunrise I was in no hurry to leave the hostel. When I did leave, I was rugged up to brace the cold wind. Over my fleece, I wore my wind and rainproof jacket. I had on gloves, a scarf and a beanie. It had stopped raining, but I had my poncho handy just in case. As I walked uphill, I watched with awe at the stunning sunrise and all around me the views were incredible. I was feeling the same sense of freedom that I had felt as I walked over the Pyrenees. I was feeling proud and courageous. I was embarking on Day 22 of my walk, and I was extremely grateful for being there right at this moment.

When I arrived at Cruz Ferro, several other pilgrims were there. I found a spot at a table and spent some time peacefully watching them as they placed down their symbols. I then decided that I would do a quick video to explain what I intended to do. The first video was about my rose quartz crystal. I planned to post this on social media. I was a little bit emotional, but I managed to deliver it. I then did a second video about the stone I was placing down for my sisters. This video was going to be kept private. I had thought maybe I might send it to each of them sometime. My sadness in that video was so intense that the video has remained private, and I have only shared it with my daughter.

WALK

After I had some time to recover from my videos, I walked over to the cross and laid down my two stones. I photographed them both in their resting spot. One represented gratitude for my incredibly fortunate life and the other, hope that conflict would end. I asked another pilgrim to take a photo of me. She was dedicated to the task and had me repose several times to get it just right. I thanked her for her commitment to making me look good.

Foncebadon to Ponferrada

The walk from Cruz Ferro through the mountains was beautiful. The rush of people from yesterday was nowhere to be seen. I was breathing in the beautiful, crisp, fresh air along the top of the mountain range while admiring the landscape. I could hear the gentle melody of cowbells in the valley. Some trees were wearing autumn colours and the contrast of the red, brown and orange leaves against the green background was vibrant. There was the occasional single flower growing in the grass and its beauty was brilliant. It was so peaceful, and I was flourishing in this environment. I didn't risk spinning around with arms open wide in case I tripped and fell down the side of the mountain, but I could relate to the opening scene of *The sound of music*. Because I was trying to take in every single moment, it probably took me much longer than it should have to walk this part of the trail today. However, walking slowly and stopping to look around me had become my mission since Day 4 when I sat on the side of the hill outside of Pamplona.

WALK

Just as I arrived to start the descent into the valley, the colour of the sky changed to a moody purple-blue as dark clouds formed above me. While it was a beautiful sight, I was hoping that the clouds were not about to grace me with a shower. That would make the steep, rocky path more difficult to navigate. I already had a lot on my mind to navigate this safely. I was being sure to use my poles effectively to stabilise my footing on the rocks and also to help carry the weight of my backpack. My fall a couple of days ago was still fresh and I didn't want to slip and fall again. There were a lot of loose rocks and I had to focus so that each step was secure. A light mist of rain was coming down and not being sure if it was going to start pouring, I was wishing that I hadn't dawdled so much on top of the mountain.

The next thing on my mind was food. I was suddenly feeling hungry. I had eaten a few crumbs of potato chips and a handful of pistachio nuts earlier, but I had eaten nothing else since breakfast. I started imagining the coffee and the food I would buy to warm me up when I reached the next town.

Almost at the bottom of my descent, Trace caught up with me. We had a great chat on our way into El Acebo. She told me that she had started the Camino journey with a friend who she had only met about five months earlier when they were working together in a mission. Unfortunately, they parted ways in the first couple of days as it was not working out. Trace said she had thought about going home but her family had encouraged her to continue. When we walked into the cafe, she stopped to talk to a couple of ladies. After we sat down inside, she said that one of those ladies was the friend she had started with.

Foncebadon to Ponferrada

The cafe was run by a young couple from Texas. They had made a big pot of chilli for lunch. I was not a fan of chilli, but the couple told me it was mild and the pilgrims sitting near me convinced me to try it. The chilli was warm and delicious and came with bread. It was just what I needed. It was a nice break from the usual ham and cheese bocadilla.

WALK

I still had a long walk to Ponferrada, so as soon as I had finished eating, I continued on my way. The rest of the walk was quite uneventful with a lot of road walking. It started to rain heavily so I had to stop and put on my poncho. In Ponferrada, I found a cosy pub opposite the old castle and booked a room. The room was a medieval style with exposed beams and dark wood.

The rain stopped temporarily, and I went back outside to walk around the castle. I took some photos and then made my way to a small convenience shop. There wasn't much to choose from, but I got some fruit, potato chips and a pastry. I wanted to order dinner somewhere, but nothing was open at that time. The kitchen in the pub was not open either so the fruit and pastry were my dinner.

Tonight was another one of great reflection about my experience at Cruz Ferro this morning. All our experiences are important as they are the elements that make our life our own. I gave blessings to all those in my past, all who are in my present and all those who will be in the future. I said an affirmation for my children, Paul and my family and slept surrounded by an aura of peace. I left my balcony window open tonight and the pouring rain lulled me to sleep.

CHAPTER 24

PONFERRADA TO VILLAFRANCA DEL BIERZO

DAY 23 – 24 KM

*'Some people walk in the rain.
Others just get wet.'*
Roger Miller

This morning the rain was hammering down. I had to adjust my packing around wet weather gear and repack the things out of my bum bag into a wet bag inside my backpack so they wouldn't get wet. I had learned this lesson way back on the Pyrenees. The change of routine made me feel disorganised. It took me longer to pack up than usual as I had to find new spots for some items. I put things in and then I took them out and changed it all again. I was clumsy and kept dropping things.

WALK

When I filled my drink bladder, I didn't tighten it up properly and it spilled on to the floor.

I rugged up for a very wet departure. It was 6 am when I left my room and stepped into the dark and pouring rain. I was in full wet weather gear. It had been weeks since I had worn the poncho. It was dark so I had my headlamp on, but the rain was so heavy I wasn't sure how far in front I would see. The first part of the walk out of Ponferrada was through a park with a river running beside it. It was isolated and had an eerie feel so I was constantly scanning around me. Before reaching the outskirts of the city, I had walked through a quiet, sleeping suburb, a hushed churchyard, an unlit tunnel, and past a very dark, shadowy cemetery. My neck was sore from constantly checking around me for dangerous strangers, ghosts or other unexpected encounters.

The walk in the rain this morning wasn't such a bad thing. I considered that it might help to wash away some of the negativity I had been carrying for the last couple of days. I had still been thinking about the big wave of pilgrims out of Astorga and the lady who was rude to me at Rabanal. This was unnecessary baggage, and the rain would help to freshen up my attitude.

I stopped at a cafe in Cabelos while it was still dark and raining. I ordered a hash brown type of pastry and drank the best coffee I had tasted so far. I should have had two of them. When I was ready to leave, I asked a pilgrim sitting at another table, to help me get my poncho over my backpack. He spoke French and didn't understand me. He was searching for straps to tie. Finally, after an exchange of single words and hand gestures, he got it and pulled the plastic over my pack.

Ponferrada to Villafranca del Bierzo

I was now about two hours into the day's walk, and I was just getting out into the country. It was starting to lighten up. Because this part of the Camino was not new to me, I was alert to searching for new things. I wanted to ensure that I was doing things differently on my solo walk so it was different from the one my daughter and I had done together. This included staying in different towns and eating at different places. I wanted to keep the memories of each Camino separate.

I stopped at a pharmacy to restock my supplies. I needed more muscle cream, anti-inflammatory tablets, pain relief tablets, antihistamine and bite cream. I was slightly embarrassed about buying so many items. I sat on the bench outside and emptied the boxes and put them in the bin so as not to be carrying all the extra weight of the packaging.

The walk had now taken me into the vineyards. There was greenery on the vines and still a few bunches of grapes here and there. I came across another blackberry bush which had some nice big, juicy blackberries. I helped myself to a handful of them for a little trail snack. They were the most delicious I had eaten so far.

It was still raining but not heavy now. There were not many pilgrims around today. Perhaps with the rain, they had delayed their start or they had decided not to walk at all. I was enjoying being out on this country road with no-one else around me. The rain had freshened everything up, including me physically and mentally. I was back in a peaceful zone. The rain on my face and my hair had worked.

Today the walk was mostly over a series of rolling hills. There were grapevines and a variety of different fruit trees along the side of the road. I came upon a pilgrim picking some figs off a tree. I stopped and asked him if they were ripe because I thought they had to change colour. He said they were great, and he gave me one to try. It was sweet. I picked myself another one. We stood for a while and chatted while we ate a few more figs. He grabbed a couple for the road and left me there while I picked some to take with me as well.

The sun came out in the last 10 minutes of the walk which, if you can believe it, was a nuisance because I had to stop and take off my rain gear and pack it away as wearing it was making me far too hot. I hadn't booked accommodation for tonight, and while that made me nervous, it indicated that I was starting to be more comfortable with taking things as they came.

I arrived in Villafranca and found a place to stay. Of course, my room was on the second floor, so I dragged myself up the old staircase. There was no wi-fi in my room, even though I checked this before I booked in. It seemed like the minute I paid for my room, the wi-fi stopped working. I skipped my routine of chores and went for a walk around town and to check where I would have to walk in the morning. I then went to a cafe to get dinner and access their wi-fi. I ordered a pilgrim's meal. It was a delicious thick soup with crusty bread, steak, and then a crème caramel for dessert. There was a carafe of red wine included. I took my time to eat so I had maximum use of the internet. I walked back to my room, showered, fussed around for a while and went to bed.

CHAPTER 25

VILLAFRANCA DEL BIERZO TO HERRERIAS

DAY 24 – 21 KM

*'Fill your life with adventures, not things.
Have stories to tell, not stuff to show.'
Unknown*

Before leaving, I went to the cafe where I ate dinner last night. I couldn't make up my mind what I wanted to eat for breakfast, so I chose a chocolate pastry out of the cabinet to have with my coffee. I wasn't so fond of the chocolate pastry but I enjoyed the coffee. I watched a few other pilgrims heading off. It was about 8 degrees this morning, but it felt colder. It wasn't raining but it had rained a lot during the night.

It was a beautiful day. I was enjoying the walk, but I was walking very slowly. I just couldn't get into a good walking rhythm which

WALK

is a major problem when one is 'walking the Camino'. I wanted to speed up, but I just couldn't despite having a good sleep last night. I felt like it was going to be a long day. My legs were sore, and I didn't feel well. I felt sleepy and unsettled. I had eaten a good meal last night so I had refuelled my body, but I could have done better at breakfast this morning. I thought I was probably more fatigued than sick.

Most of the walk was on the main road. On one side was a river and the sound of the river flowing was relaxing and compensated for the sound of the cars. At the entry to the village of Pereje, there were two men with buckets. They were collecting the chestnuts that had fallen from the trees which lined the road. There were hundreds of them on the ground. The prickly and furry chestnut cases fall to the ground and then split open for the reddish-brown nut to fall out.

I needed a bathroom stop, so I went into a cafe and ordered an orange juice. I used the bathroom and then I sat outside and had my orange juice and ate some snacks from my stash. I was not keen to get moving again. I continued back out on to the country road. There was a lot of mist covering the mountains and the rain was still holding off. I loved hearing the pretty music of the cow bells as the cows ate grass or moved around.

I walked towards a cow paddock and further up on the road, a farmer was trying to get his cows to go through a gate. They were not cooperating and suddenly, they turned and started running towards me. At first, I stepped back against the barb wire fence, but I knew that this was as far as I would be able to go and the 10 cows coming my way did not look like they were going to stop and walk gently past me. I made a split-second decision to run to the other side of the road. It probably wasn't much of a run with

Villafranca del Bierzo to Herrerias

my backpack, my fatigue, and my sore legs slowing me down, but I was moving as quickly as I could. The cows continued up the road with the farmer chasing behind them. Someone else had jumped in their car and was trying to get in front of them to stop their run. After they had passed, I wished I had turned on my GoPro because it would have been terrific filming all these cows running at me.

I arrived at my pre-booked accommodation. It was a little chalet and was at the bottom of the mountain range I would be confronting tomorrow. The manager said that he did not have my booking. I looked at him in desperation. I didn't want to turn around and go back to the previous town and the next village ahead of me was small and may not have any accommodation available. I was prepared to disguise begging in friendly conversation for any space he could find for me. To my absolute joy, he had a room for me. He said he always keeps one free just in case this situation arises. Luck or charm it did not matter. I was grateful for my warm, cosy room with a country décor of polished wood and floral linens.

After I had settled in, I headed down to the dining room and ordered a big bowl of spaghetti. I was so hungry that I ate it very quickly. Just as I finished it the American couple came in. They were staying in the small village up ahead. The hostel they were staying in was not serving any food as they were closing tomorrow. The peak season for pilgrims was over and many of the albergues in small villages were shutting.

I joined Carol and Jeremy at their table and while they ate their meal, I had a couple of glasses of wine. We talked for ages. I learned that Carol was originally from Peru. She was in her 60s but looked nothing like it. She had almost flawless skin. Jeremy was also in his 60s. He had a calming presence and a warm tone

WALK

to his voice. He said they had seen me at Cruz Ferro and noticed that I was upset. I told them the story about my two stones. After a couple of hours catching up, we said good night and I headed up to my room for a much needed sleep in preparation to 'beat the mountain that beat me last time'.

CHAPTER 26

HERRERIAS TO TRIACASTELA

DAY 25 – 26 KM

'Today is your day.
Your mountain is waiting.
So, get on your way.'
Dr Seuss

It was dark, cold and raining as I departed this morning. I was heading to O'Cebreiro to tackle the mountain that had left me completely traumatised last time I was here. I had intended to eat breakfast where I had stayed but it was 7:30 am and the kitchen still wasn't open. I didn't want to wait any longer, so I walked to the main part of the village. There was a cafe open, and I got a coffee and a hot muffin. After the big bowl of spaghetti last night, I wasn't very hungry. The top of my feet were sore this morning. This was a new pain. The muscles in my legs were slightly sore but I hoped they would warm up soon.

WALK

I walked for half an hour uphill on a bitumen road while it was still dark. I took off my poncho as the rain had stopped. I was starting to think that in the dark, I might have missed the turnoff from the bitumen road to the track that went up the side of the mountain. I walked a bit further and thankfully it was there. I mouthed to myself, 'Let the pain commence'. This might have seemed a bit negative but last time I was here, the mountain chewed me up and spat me out into the snow. I was remembering the two days I had spent here last year.

The first time I walked up this mountain, I was on the final stretch of Day 4 of my Camino walk. I was not anywhere as fit then as I was now on Day 25. That day, I struggled to get up the steep incline. Then just to make it harder, about halfway up there was heavy snow and, in some parts, it was knee-deep. When we were almost at the top, we were hit with pounding rain (or maybe it was sleet) and then the hail came down. We scrambled to get to the top and came into a snow-covered village. We hadn't booked accommodation, so we had to go door to door asking if there were any rooms available. There was nothing and the only option left was the very large albergue.

We entered the albergue soaking wet and miserable. This was to be our first albergue stay so we didn't know what we were in for. We were allocated a room number and a bunk bed each. We headed to our room and saw that we were to share a room with about fifty other pilgrims. I went to the shower first and to my horror, there were no doors on the showers. I went into the one right at the end of the row and showered very quickly and then dressed. After Chelsea had her shower, we went out to find somewhere to eat.

We found a place that was like a tavern. It was small and crowded but it had a wood fire, so we were happy. We ordered soup and

Herrerias To Triacastela

with it came the regular basket of crusty bread. It was delicious. We delayed our departure from this warm room as much as possible before we had to go back out into the snow to return to the albergue. Eventually, we decided that it must be done. To say that our night of sleep was miserable would not be an exaggeration.

In the morning we woke up early and dragged our gear into the hallway and packed up to leave. When we walked out into the darkness, we were not sure where to go. After searching around looking for an arrow, we headed off. We were walking uphill, in knee-deep snow, in the dark, with only myself wearing a headlamp. Chelsea was following me and halfway up, one of my poles snapped. Chelsea gave me one of hers and she struggled on with one. We had no idea if we were on the edge of a mountain or not, or even the direction of where we were going.

After tackling this part of the walk, we came to an intersection leading to a bitumen road. It was still dark, and we just had to guess which way to go. Thankfully, we made the right choice. There was plenty of snow around us and we decided to abandon the Camino path and stay on the road. The hours of walking in the rain and cold wind that followed that day pushed us to our limit. To describe that day as woeful would be an understatement. When we arrived at the town where we were staying that night, we were exhausted and traumatised.

This time, I was confident that it would be different. I was determined to win the battle and claim the victory. I enjoyed the serenity of the first part of the climb through the canopy-covered path which was wet and muddy from the rain this morning. I was surrounded by large trees, fernery and plants. I could hear raindrops still falling from the taller trees onto the smaller plants and ferns which kept the path damp. There were slippery leaves

WALK

to watch for and I had to be cautious to keep my balance as I walked over stones which were not only wet but covered in moss. It was challenging but I was happy to bathe in the beauty of this natural environment.

I came to a village, and I thought I must have almost reached the top of the mountain. I went into a cafe and ordered a coffee. I sat and casually drank it thinking I was about to be crowned 'queen of the mountain', but it turned out to be a false celebration. I was in for a surprise because I realised that I was probably only halfway to the top.

It had become colder and windier as I went higher but it was not raining. I came to the statue that marks the border into the Galician area. I decided that I had time to take a selfie with the statue. While I was setting up my GoPro on its stand, a couple of female pilgrims walked past. I was immediately intimidated about taking a selfie and so I stopped. Because I was stopped there, they stopped and seemed to be looking around to see what they were missing. I was like, 'Nothing to see here guys. I am just having a few potato chips.' Not finding anything wonderful worth noticing, they went on their way. I quickly took my selfie in case someone else came along.

From here the wind started to pick up. It was blowing the smaller trees around. The wind was icy, and my hands were freezing but I was busy taking photos and film so I did not put on my gloves. Just around the corner, there was a beautiful view overlooking the valley and the next row of mountains. I set the GoPro up on the side of the path and stepped back towards the edge. I used my remote and clicked some photos. I was showing the mountain that I was in charge this time. Just as I put the GoPro away, the wind started raging and the rain started falling. I grabbed my poncho and put it on. I could not believe how suddenly it picked up. The

Herrerias To Triacastela

mountain was returning the message and telling me it was still in charge, and I, definitely, was not.

By the time I walked into O'Cebreiro, the wind was a gale, and the rain was so heavy I could barely see where I was going. I went straight to the tavern where we had eaten the delicious soup last year. I walked in dripping wet and enquired if they had any soup. I was happy to see the fire going. While I savoured a bowl of warm soup, the two ladies at the counter had an animated discussion in Spanish. I guessed they might be talking about these crazy pilgrims who think it is fun to walk in this weather. When I had finished, I thanked the ladies and rugged up ready to go outside. The rain had stopped but the poncho remained in an easy to reach spot. I walked to the edge of the road and took a couple of photos. I was satisfied because the weather had cleared enough for me to see the view.

The next part of the walk was fascinating. It had been a challenge in the dark and the snow last year but today, it was a beautiful path

WALK

through a forest. There were blackberry plants, a distinct type of pine tree, and all sorts of different sized, coloured mushrooms. The path was on the side of the mountain, so Chelsea and I were extremely lucky that we had managed to stay in the centre of the path on that dark, snowy morning a year earlier and not veer to the right. When I came to the familiar bitumen road intersection, the wind was blowing furiously, and the big trees were swaying. The rain came down hard and felt like shards of ice were hitting my face. I promptly put on my poncho and gloves. It wasn't long before one side of my face started to feel numb from the cold. I pulled my jacket hood down as far as it would go. I had my visor under the hood so that the top of the hood was raised, and I could still see where to go. I was cold and not having much fun.

Jeremy and Carol caught up to me as I walked into a village. There was a cafe, so we decided to go inside and get out of the rain and cold for a while. It was crowded with other pilgrims who had the same idea. I ordered coffee and soup. Jeremy and I had a deep conversation about a range of things. I told him a couple of stories about myself and at one point he sat back and said, 'Michelle. You have got to cut yourself some slack sometimes. If you do this, everything will still be okay.'

This led to a discussion about the concept of making reasonable decisions. Jeremy explained to me that sometimes we need to evaluate and re-evaluate what we are doing and when there is a decision to be made it doesn't matter what anyone thinks but yourself, and at that point, you must make the reasonable decision that works for you. He told me a story about when he was faced with a big decision and how his friend had said to him that he had to weigh it up, and while it may not be perfect, if it was reasonable, it would be okay.

Herrerias To Triacastela

We talked about setting goals. Most people set a range of big goals, small goals and daily goals. We explored the idea that the purpose of setting goals was to avoid the concept of death. When we no longer have goals, it may mean that we have nothing further to do. I had not anticipated this discussion today but it was probably the most thought-provoking one I had ever had.

Despite the cafe being warm and comfortable and the good company I was with, I knew that I had to get going again as I still had about three hours to walk. It was miserable outside, but my thoughts were now consumed with these new ideas Jeremy and I had discussed. I thought back to this conversation about a week later when I had to make a reasonable decision.

I walked the next three hours in the freezing, cold rain. It was getting darker, and I hurried as much as I could. I had booked accommodation in Triacastela and I was glad to arrive.

CHAPTER 27

TRIACASTELA TO BARBADELO

DAY 26 – 23 KM

*'The charm of a woodland road,
Lies not only in its beauty,
but in anticipation.'
Dale Rex Coman*

This morning I was really, really tired and not very enthusiastic. It was very dark, cold and wet. I had to stay alert to find the Camino signs I needed to follow. I had no idea where I was and was frantically searching for a sign to tell me that I was on the right path. I had already walked through two little hamlets. There was no sign of any other humans. The only sign of life was a rooster crowing, some owls hooting, and a lot of cowbells in the paddocks beside me. When I finally saw a sign that said, 'Go this way', I went that way without questioning it. I knew that I was on a steep, rocky incline. It was probably good that I was still walking in the dark because I couldn't see how hard it was. But I could feel it. My feet were touchy and there was the occasional sharp pain.

Daylight was breaking as I reached the top of the mountain. There was a heavy mist around and I could see the twinkle of scattered lights in the little villages on the mountainside and in the valley. The birds had come out to the edge of the road and were playing in the puddles. The paddocks were green and grassy. It was dairy country. On either side of the road, was a forest. The wind was blowing through the branches and leaves were falling all around me like snow.

I was enjoying being here on my own. Even if you choose to walk the Camino with another person or a group, I recommend you find a way to walk in solitude for some of the time. It will give you some moments of quietness where you can go deep into your thoughts.

In the city of Sarria, I stopped at a trekking equipment shop to get some new stoppers for the ends of my walking poles. The current rubber ends had worn out and the constant clicking on the bitumen was annoying. Next stop was to buy some lunch and go to the bathroom. The lady who made my bocadilla wrapped it up carefully for me to take away. The bocadilla was so big, I was worried that I would not have space to carry it. It was the size of half a loaf of bread and was filled with ham and cheese. I planned to eat lunch once I was on the other side of Sarria.

There was a nice forest walk after Sarria. There were stunning big trees, and the trunks were twisted in unusual shapes. While I was walking through here and admiring the trees, a pilgrim from Ireland and one from Sweden greeted me. We stopped and chatted for a while. They noticed my knee guards and asked how my knees

Triacastela to Barbadelo

were holding up. I said that my knees were doing well but it was my feet that were bad. I said I was now having to take quite a few painkillers to ease the pain. The pilgrim from Sweden said he was forced to take the train from Fromista to Leon and had rested there for four days because his shins were so painful. He said he too was relying on pain medication to keep going.

It made me think about a conversation between myself, Jeremy, Carol, and the manager from the chalet where I had stayed in Herrerias. We were talking about some pilgrims that had booked a horse ride up to O'Cebreiro, instead of walking. The manager said the Camino is recognised by walking, bike and horse. Jeremy added, 'Taxi, bus, train, anything'. We laughed at this, but this is what happens. If you need a taxi, bus, or train, or if you need pain medication and knee braces to make it as enjoyable and manageable as possible to finish, then do it. As Jeremy would say 'make reasonable choices'. Do whatever allows you to continue.

At Barbadelo, I saw an albergue right at the side of the road. It seemed busy but I was ready to stop. I asked for a private room, and I was lucky enough to get one. If they hadn't had a private room available, I would have kept walking. I went up to my room to drop off my gear and then went back down to the reception area as I had forgotten to ask for the wi-fi password. I ordered a beer and read my guidebook to get a sense of where I might stay over the next couple of nights. I did plan to eat at the restaurant, but it was so busy I changed my mind. I bought some food from the cafe and returned to my room. I chose one of my three single beds and had a very peaceful sleep.

The Camino was getting busier. Sarria was the starting place for pilgrims who only wanted to walk the last 100 kilometres of the Camino, or they had a very short time frame in which to walk.

CHAPTER 28

BARBADELO TO GONZAR

DAY 27 – 26 KM

'We no longer build fireplaces for physical warmth.
We build them for the warmth of the soul.
We build them to dream by and to hope by.'
Edna Ferber

I left at 6:30 am. It was not raining now but it had been overnight. It was a very cold morning and I was rugged up in my jacket, scarf, fleece and gloves. The wind on my face was strong and cold. Once I started walking, I warmed up pretty quickly. It was another very dark start to the day and I followed the path through an alley of trees. I wasn't nervous but I was on high alert. Mostly for dogs.

The place I stayed in last night, started serving breakfast at 6:30 am. I wanted to leave before this, so I planned to stop at the next

WALK

town. Some pilgrims prefer to sleep in and have their breakfast and coffee before they leave their accommodation. Some just don't like to walk in the dark. It was my personal preference. I loved being out in the country when day broke, and I witnessed nature waking up around me.

Walking into the village of Morgade, I could smell the wood fires. This was becoming more common in the villages as the mornings were cooling down. It made me feel homesick. We had an open fireplace at home when I was growing up. I have five siblings and we would spend a lot of time around the fire in winter, hanging out with friends, listening to music, toasting marshmallows and watching television. To me, a fireplace represents a family coming together and my thoughts were focused on the cosiness and safety of being with family, at home. After almost a month of walking on my own, I was missing the comfort of home more and more each day.

As the sun rose, I could see beautiful green grassy paddocks with stone fences separating them. My big reward for walking for a few hours in the dark this morning was being right in the middle of a dairy when a herd of cows came in for milking. There was a large cow in front of me refusing to move and the farmer was becoming angry and waving his arms at the cow. The cow stubbornly stood its ground for some time before finally following the farmer's instructions and moving to the milking area.

It had been a beautiful morning and I had completed two hours of walking. Every day there were plenty of chestnuts lying on the path. This furry red carpet added to the ambience of the walk. I had snacked on a few dried figs and had drunk plenty of water but I was starting to feel like I needed something else to eat. Just after walking through the dairy, I came across a little cafe right

Barbadelo to Gonzar

on my path. I sat outside and had a coffee and a piece of Galician cake while I looked out to the beautiful country. A light mist was resting over the paddocks.

Directly opposite the cafe, was a Camino stone marker that indicated I had 102 kilometres to walk to Santiago de Compostela. Feeling a rush of pride, I left the cafe. I had 100 kilometres to go. While I gazed at the beauty of the morning and thought about what I had achieved up to here, a couple of tears dripped down my cheeks.

It wasn't long before a light, misty rain started to fall. I stopped and put my rainproof jacket on and covered my backpack with its waterproof jacket. As I came out of the woodland and into a village, I saw a 'gang' of four dogs coming directly towards me. My adrenalin started surging. There was nowhere for me to hide. I moved right over to the edge of the path, pulled my visor down, and kept walking. I was doing my best to try and not appear to be threatening and I hoped they just wouldn't notice me. To my relief, they took no notice of me and just kept on walking.

I was walking well today. I was feeling an energy pulling me forward. I was now about three days walk from Santiago and I was spending some time thinking about whether I wanted to walk into Santiago in the morning or the afternoon. I continued to contemplate this over the next few days and would decide as I got closer to Santiago.

That afternoon, I stopped at a guesthouse in a very small village. The lady who checked me in frightened me a little. She was Spanish and she spoke very little English. She came across as quite stern and guarded and I would not describe her as friendly. She was over 6 feet tall and had an intimidating presence. I asked her about

WALK

somewhere to get food and she said there was a place up the road. I thought it could be a mile away and because I was so tired and it was rainy and dark, I decided that I wouldn't go anywhere. I had a fine selection of snacks for dinner including a chocolate bar, a handful of potato chips and a little bottle of Baileys left in my snack stash. So that was dinner.

CHAPTER 29

GONZAR TO MELIDE

DAY 28 – 32 KM

*'I'd rather be hiking in the rain,
than sitting inside at a desk on a sunny day.'
Unknown*

I had not slept well. It was cold and rain fell heavy on the window all night. There were street lights streaming in through the window directly onto the bed. A dog was continually barking and there were two flies in the room buzzing constantly throughout the night. I dozed in and out of sleep and when I woke up this morning, I didn't feel very rested.

I had a very hot shower to warm up and I dressed in my full rain gear. When I stepped out of the guesthouse it was extremely dark and pouring rain. My headlamp was barely cutting through the rain. It was no surprise that everything was wet and there was either mud or big puddles to walk through. I was hungry and I was tired and definitely not feeling enthusiastic about today's upcoming adventure.

Once I walked out of Gonzar, I had no idea where I was supposed to go. I had made it out to the highway but I wasn't feeling comfortable and it was so dark. I had to walk right on the very edge of the road and there was a lot of traffic for that time of the morning. The trucks worried me the most. They were so fast and I seemed to be right beside them when they passed. I had a Camino symbol on the back of my poncho that lit up in the light and I was hoping that would be protecting me a little from the traffic behind. I only had my headlamp to warn the oncoming traffic. The frustration I was feeling for the traffic, rain, darkness and no sense of direction, provoked a couple of inappropriate words. The conditions were terrible and I didn't know for sure that I was going the right way.

My headlamp flashed on to a stop sign. I wondered if this was a sign that I should stop and wait until it was light. At one point, I followed a little track that ran off from the side of the highway. I stayed on it for about 500 metres but decided to come back onto the highway as I wasn't sure where it was heading. I kept telling myself that once I found somewhere for breakfast, my spirits might lift but right now I was battling to stay optimistic. There was no joy in this morning for me. It was really, really difficult. In my head, I found myself questioning why on earth any sane person would think it was a good idea to be trudging along a highway in Spain, in the morning darkness and the pouring rain, just hoping that they were heading in the right direction.

I continued in the direction I thought I should go until I found a Camino sign which directed me off to the side of the highway. I felt much safer. When I finally reached a cafe it was still raining

Gonzar to Melide

and dark. I ordered a ham and cheese omelette and a coffee. After eating I felt much better. When I left the cafe, daybreak was emerging. The rain continued to fall but at least I could see now.

I still had 27 kilometres to walk from here and I had already experienced a vast range of emotions in the first few hours of this morning. I had gone from exhausted, to tired, to uninterested. I had been confused, lost and scared. It was just one of those days. I was now three days from reaching Santiago. While it had not been a very good morning, I was doing okay. My body was tired and I was well aware that I had to be cautious not to upscale the little challenges into big challenges. Now, more than ever, was the time to pull myself together and get on with it.

The road from the cafe led into a forest. On one side of me was eucalypt and on the other was pine. The rain on these trees created an aroma-therapeutic scent. I took advantage of this natural restoration, slowed down and breathed in the smell of wet wood, damp soil, eucalypt and pine. I started to relax and regain some positivity.

Today was the most mentally challenging day I had experienced up to this point. It was extremely hard to find any amount of joy. I was dripping wet despite waterproof gear and it just got colder as the day progressed. It was hard to stay on my feet and keep going. It poured non-stop all day and I was freezing cold. There was so much water, that my waterproof boots were wet through and my socks were squishy. My body felt like it was full of water, and I was wading through a river. It was positively quiet on the path with very few pilgrims joining me. I guessed the ones I didn't see were the smart ones because they were not in this torrential rain. A lot of taxis were rushing past and some may have chosen to take the quick and dry way to their next town.

WALK

Today was more difficult than Day 17 when I walked on the Roman road. I had to source every ounce of determination to keep going. I put my head down and pushed through and when I finally arrived in Melide, I was thoroughly soaked and dripping water from everywhere. I was so pleased that I had packed all my gear in waterproof plastic bags and today that had paid off, so things in my backpack remained dry. I was cold and looking forward to a hot meal and a shower. When I got to my room, I was impressed to find that not only did it have heating, it also had a heated floor. I turned the floor heat up and laid my clothes out to dry on the hottest part of the floor. There was a hairdryer. It was nice to have dry hair after the constant dripping today. When I had finished my chores, I went back downstairs and ordered a pilgrim's meal and wine.

My last thoughts before sleep were imagining that I was sitting on my big comfy couch at home, wrapped in my memory blanket from Canada, holding a red wine and watching a favourite movie.

CHAPTER 30

MELIDE TO O PEDROUZO

DAY 29 – 33 KM

*'Don't let yesterday,
take up too much of today.'*
Will Rogers

I did not have any quality sleep last night. I wasn't sure if my room was next to a nightclub or people were partying in other rooms around me. There was party music playing until about 5 am. I put in my earphones to listen to relaxing music and that helped me doze in and out of sleep. I dragged myself out of my room at about 8 am. I had big day ahead of me with a 33-kilometre walk. This morning, the path led straight into a eucalypt forest which was veiled with mist. It was very muddy. I was surrounded by fog and there was a light, dewy rain. The large trees were domineering and majestic in their stature and form. The birds were in full song.

WALK

Melide to O Pedrouzo

Because of the beauty around me, I was relaxed and enjoying my surroundings.

I realised today, that my clothes were starting to have that damp smell that was hard to wash out. It was from the amount of time not fully dry in the morning when I had packed them. I had been wearing them for almost a month now. They needed a thorough wash. For the time being, I made sure to put on lots of deodorant to mask the smell from others and myself.

Today was one of the prettiest walks of the whole Camino. It was an enchanting gift. There were many subtle blessings and moments during today's walk. The weather had varied between sunshine, fog, rain, showers and mist. There were cows, roosters, hens, ducks, goats and birds. There were beautiful flowers and gardens, cute cottages, pretty little creeks and medieval bridges. The eucalypt trees were stunning, and the smell was incredible. I found some houses for sale along the way. They needed a bit of work (like a roof and doors) but they were going cheap.

Despite it being a beautiful landscape, because of my tiredness, it was a very, very long and slow day for me. The last few kilometres felt like I was walking on razor blades. However, at the same time, I was incredibly happy and joyful. I had moments of tears because the wonder of the day was truly magnificent. Today I had been 'forest bathing'. This is an eco-therapy that involves immersing yourself in nature. It benefits physical, mental, emotional and social health and improves stress levels because positive hormones are released. My positive hormones were certainly released today and with one day's walk to Santiago left, it was perfect timing.

I arrived in O Pedrouzo and located my room in a guesthouse. I was greeted with chocolate and a ginger beer. The room was

WALK

warm and wonderfully comfortable. I turned the heating up. The lady who owned the guest house brought me a pack of goodies later that afternoon. This would be my snack tomorrow. It was a nice little extra and I was very appreciative.

I was excited about tomorrow when I would walk into Santiago. It was hard to believe that I had been walking for 29 days and it was almost over. Physically, I was in bad shape. My body had taken a bit of a beating and to its credit had still kept going and got me here. My mind had been a roller-coaster of thoughts and emotions and had weathered the mental challenges of a solo walk. My resilience was tested, but had survived in reasonable shape. One more day. Santiago here I come.

CHAPTER 31

O PEDROUZO TO SANTIAGO DE COMPOSTELA

DAY 30 – 20 KM

*'Travelling alone will be the scariest,
most liberating,
life-changing experience of your life.
Try it at least once.'*
Unknown

Emotions cascaded as I walked into Santiago and saw the spires of the cathedral. I had entered this city before with my daughter, but the feeling of achievement today was overwhelming. This time it was a solitary event.

WALK

As before, there was no welcoming party or cheering crowds on the sidelines. There was no painted yellow line to step over and no-one handing out ribbons or medals. The finish line of the Camino walk for me was peaceful and humble. I arrived in the plaza and stood still looking up at the cathedral. Internally, I congratulated myself and said well done. I was pleased and satisfied with my strength of determination, resilience and power of positive thought.

I took off my backpack and sat there for a while and reflected on my journey. I had walked 790 kilometres on my own. It is difficult to describe fully this feeling. Each day of walking had provided new and different challenges. I had pushed myself physically and mentally to my limits and while there were times I was completely overwhelmed, I had continued and finished what I set out to do. I had relied on my determination to keep going and I wasn't sure how I had kept going on some days.

As I sat there and took in the scene around me, Josh walked up to me. It was great to see him. We talked about how we had each found the walk since we had seen each other. Josh offered to take some photos of me in front of the cathedral and I gladly accepted. He arrived the day before and had already taken his photos. We discussed our plans for the next few days. We were both planning to continue walking to Finisterre. We thought that we probably would see each other over the next few days so I said goodbye and went to find my accommodation.

Although I had officially finished my Camino walk, I was planning that tomorrow morning, I would commence walking to Finisterre. I went down to the post office to collect the items I had sent on from Astorga. I booked accommodation for when I returned to Santiago in a couple of days. I took out from my backpack, anything

O Pedrouzo to Santiago de Compostela

that I thought I could do without for a couple of days and put it in a separate bag. I then took that bag and my post office parcel to the guesthouse where I would be staying when I came back from Finisterre. The guesthouse staff said they would be happy to look after it for me.

I wandered around Santiago for a while. The cathedral was undergoing internal repairs and was not open. Fortunately, I had gone inside last year and attended the pilgrim's mass.

WALK

Attending the mass was a formal way to end the Camino walk. The Botafumeiro was swinging that year and the experience of being there with Chelsea, and other pilgrims I had met along the way, was wonderful. Next year was a Holy Year, so the church was being renovated to prepare for the celebrations.

I finished my afternoon of sightseeing and bought myself a silver charm for my bangle. It was two little boots and it would go with my Camino shell from last year. I bought some dinner and then headed back to my room.

My plan tomorrow morning was to have a hot shower, pack up, eat a big breakfast, and then head off for the start of my holiday. I was keen to walk to the 'end of the world' where the Atlantic Ocean met the shore at Finisterre. I was looking forward to eating some seafood and enjoying a holiday at the beach. I imagined I would walk into Finisterre triumphantly holding up my walking poles and revelling in a glorious end to my adventure. Of course, I had no idea that my arrival at Finisterre was not going to be the celebration I was imagining. The Universe had a different plan.

CHAPTER 32

SANTIAGO DE COMPOSTELA TO FINISTERRE

DAY 31

*'Maybe there are no lessons.
Things just are.'*
Unknown

I had a sleep in this morning and then a nice, hot shower. I ate breakfast and then departed at 8:30 am. It was a cool morning and I was glad that there was no rain. It felt like Day 1 of a holiday. I was looking forward to getting to the beach, but I still had two days of walking ahead of me, which I thought should be a breeze. Today was only a short 20 kilometre walk. I was surprised at how many other pilgrims were headed off with me this morning. Once out of the city, it was a fairly relaxing walk. It was pretty and I was

WALK

enjoying the morning. I realised that I was just dawdling along. Unintentionally, I was taking it as a recovery day. Most of the human pilgrim traffic had gone past me.

After a couple of hours of walking, my feet had become sore again and I was tired so I stopped to have lunch. I sat down at a busy cafe and looking around realised that I did not recognise a single person. I was once again in a new pilgrim tribe. I finished lunch and then walked to the pharmacy next door for some supplies and took time to rub some more muscle cream on my feet.

It was not long after this, that everything changed. I was halfway through the day and unexpectedly, I had to walk up a very steep hill. It was very challenging and I was surprised that I found it so difficult even with my poles out to help. I should have easily walked up that hill but my feet were sore and I was fatigued.

I was midway through the hill when I stopped. I just decided then and there that I didn't want to do this anymore. Here was the Forrest Gump moment that I had talked about with Josh. I didn't want to walk anymore. I didn't want to talk to anyone. I didn't want to meet new pilgrims. I wanted to get out of these clothes and get a clean outfit. All of a sudden, I was sick of being a pilgrim.

So, here I was. I still had about eight kilometres to walk to get to the town where I was supposed to stay tonight. I was walking beside a main road and I was shedding tears. All I could think about was going home and being with my patient, caring partner who supported my crazy idea to walk this solo adventure. I wanted to see my children and my family. However, I had no choice but to continue to walk these last kilometres. I thought that if I just kept going, putting one painful foot in front of the other, this feeling would dissipate, and I would be okay again.

Santiago de Compostela to Finisterre

I did not want to be defeated. I didn't want to say that I hadn't finished exactly what I set out to do. I equated that with failure. I had always been prepared to do things the hard way because I wanted to encourage others that anything was possible if you put in the effort. I thought I would let down all the people who were following me and were expecting me to arrive at Finisterre with the gloriously orchestrated finish I had planned. Most of all, I thought I would be letting down myself.

My thoughts went back to my conversation with Jeremy. I could hear him say, 'Girl you need to cut yourself some slack and make a reasonable decision for yourself.' He would have told me that nobody was going to care if I stopped walking and that there was no need to push myself any further. One less pilgrim on the trail would mean nothing. I did not have to keep going. This was not failure. It was a win. I had walked hundreds of kilometres on my own and now I could decide to stop if I wanted.

I was overwhelmed and barely holding it together. I had to start thinking differently. My thoughts raced. Isn't this part of the Camino my holidays? Why am I walking? I had to adapt my thinking so that this became an easy, enjoyable last couple of days. I should not be feeling defeated. I should be feeling excited and proud. I had accomplished a wonderful goal and I was now about to make a 'reasonable' decision.

I pushed on and did the best I could. My feet felt broken and I was reduced to a hobble. I was extremely tired and felt completely worn out from the overall challenge of the last month. I limped into Najera and checked in at my hotel. I knew what I had to do.

I decided that in the morning, I would catch a taxi to Finisterre to start the holiday that I had been looking forward to. Once the

WALK

decision was made, I relaxed. I had a warm bath, tended to my broken feet, and went down to the dining room for dinner. I was looking forward to arriving at the beach tomorrow.

CHAPTER 33

FINISTERRE

DAY 32

THE END OF THE WORLD AND THE END OF MY CAMINO

*'Maybe the journey isn't so much about becoming anything.
Maybe it's about un-becoming everything that isn't really you,
so you can be who you were meant to be in the first place.'*
Paul Coelho

I realised that the Camino isn't a journey. It is a series of moments, which form days, that when combined end in a destination. When taking time to focus or reflect, it was surprising to discover that the smallest of those moments had the greatest meaning. These moments compelled me to observe and think about things that I might otherwise have ignored. The combination of daily moments truly became more significant than the final arrival at the destination.

WALK

I didn't walk the Camino to run away from my day-to-day life, find myself or heal from a trauma. But somehow it did all of that. Did it change me? In conversation with others, I would play that down and firmly answer no. But it has changed me. How? I can't articulate it. But I feel it. Since my return from the Camino, I feel grounded and content. I prioritise wellness and peace and they are now a part of my purpose and flow.

On the Camino, I had plenty of time to think about what is important to me. Each day there was a new impromptu lesson in the meaning of life. In times of profound emotion (which was often), there was no need to think about it, I could feel it, deep inside.

The reciprocity of kindness and good natured and pleasant exchanges between strangers are to key to surviving this experience. The Camino demonstrates these two essential elements every day.

As I walked, the days of solitude and quiet nurtured my soul, cleansed my spirit, and detoxed my body. My eyes were dedicated to nature and colour. Never before had I examined the changing ground I walked on, admired the creation of forests, rivers or mountains, appreciated the brilliantly coloured skies, noticed a variety of distinct plants, trees and animals, marvelled at the formation of clouds, respected the nuances of weather, or engaged in deep conversation with strangers.

Even though I witnessed incredible landscapes and big views, it was the little things that were magnified and highlighted. I often walked resiliently in tough weather conditions, but it was the times when I was still, that I felt unexpected emotions fully. The most surprising of all were the times when, in moments of unintended mindfulness, I felt my spirit lift and my heart fill with pure joy.

Finisterre

In Finisterre, I waded in the water of the Atlantic Ocean, in the early morning. The soothing sounds of the gentle waves on the beach reminded me of how much I loved water. The cold water was a welcome tonic for my aching feet and felt like the last ritual to clear away the dust, put closure to the difficult parts of solo travel and ready my body to start anew at whatever came my way.

In the afternoon, I sat on the rocks at Finisterre and looked out to the Atlantic Ocean. It really did feel like I was sitting at the 'end of the world'. I was proud of what I had achieved and it didn't matter that there was no-one else there to witness it. I felt deep emotion and gratitude and I was thankful for the experience. As I looked at the vast ocean reaching to the horizon, I thought about the days that had challenged me and the lessons I had learned. I could list off many moments that could be considered lessons, but maybe they weren't lessons. Maybe they are just moments; gifts of beauty, inspiration, imagination, wonder and joy. I leave this Camino with a full heart and knowing that if I do nothing else, I have done enough.

WALK

I hope you have been inspired to set goals you thought were beyond your reach and that despite your doubts and fears, you will go ahead with enthusiasm and courage to achieve what you didn't think was possible.
'Buen Camino'

ABOUT THE AUTHOR

Michelle Fraser is a proud mother of two adult children and partner to an extraordinary man.

Although introverted in nature, Michelle embraces challenge and change. She is creative and thinks big, but is generally quiet and reflective.

Her curious, adventurous nature means she always takes time to experience the unfamiliar and along the way has had some epic adventures including treks to Mt Everest, Tibet, Nepal, Cambodia, Thailand and Malaysia.

Michelle mustered her adventurous, gypsy spirit and in September 2019, she set off on a solo walk of 850 kilometres along the Camino Frances in Spain to see and experience the unfamiliar. She departed from Saint Jean Pied de Port in France, crossed the Pyrenees mountains and continued across the top of Spain to Finisterre on the edge of the Atlantic Ocean. This was a solo walk over a 32-day period.

Along the way, Michelle realised that the Camino is not a journey; it is a series of moments, which form days, that when combined, end in a destination. It challenged Michelle's mind and body. She was surprised and rewarded with unexpected moments of

WALK

interaction and surprising sights. She was profoundly influenced by some revealing conversations with fellow pilgrims.

When taking time to focus or reflect, it was surprising to discover that the smallest of those moments had the greatest meaning. These moments, compelled Michelle to observe and think about things that she might otherwise have ignored. The combination of daily moments truly became more significant than the final arrival at the destination.

MICHELLE FRASER

is the author of Walk - Unexpected adventures on the Camino.

She is a mother of two adult children, has enjoyed a lifetime career as an educator, and loves adventures and challenges that spark new learning and perspectives. Although introverted, quiet and reflective, Michelle relishes the feeling of being out of her comfort zone because this is where she experiences the moments that lift her spirit and satisfy her curiosity.

Michelle speaks from the heart when she tells the honest and raw story of her adventures. Michelle walked the Camino Frances, almost 850 km, across the top of Spain on her own. This walk was not a journey, but a series of moments that when combined, ended in a destination. The combination of daily moments truly became more significant than the final destination. Michelle challenged her body, examined her soul and learnt the feeling of living in the moment.

Michelle believes that everyone can set a goal and achieve it. It doesn't have to be a trek across Spain, but something else that pulls you out of your comfort zone. Once achieved, it can empower you to meet the challenges you face in everyday life. Despite our assumed limitations, we are all capable of accomplishing more than we can imagine.

Michelle will talk about how to:

1. Live your life with Intention
- Identify what sets your soul on fire
- Discover how small adventures have as much value as the big ones

2. Be Brave
- Do something you have always wanted to do
- Reduce fears and doubts with strong plans

3. Focus on the Moments not the Destination
- Slow down
- Make reasonable decisions
- Acquire wisdom, confidence and gratitude

To enquire about booking Michelle to speak at your next event, contact her on michelletfraser29@gmail.com

REFLECTIONS

WALK

Reflections

WALK

Reflections

www.ingramcontent.com/pod-product-compliance
Lightning Source LLC
Chambersburg PA
CBHW030053100526
44591CB00008B/129